Life
LOVES
You

Also by Louise Hay

BOOKS/KIT

All Is Well (with Mona Lisa Schulz, M.D., Ph.D.)
Colors & Numbers
Empowering Women
Everyday Positive Thinking
Experience Your Good Now!
A Garden of Thoughts: My Affirmation Journal
Gratitude: A Way of Life (Louise & Friends)
Heal Your Body
Heal Your Body A–Z
Heart Thoughts (also available in a gift edition)
I Can Do It® (book-with-CD)
Inner Wisdom
Letters to Louise
Life! Reflections on Your Journey
Love Your Body
Love Yourself, Heal Your Life Workbook
Loving Yourself to Great Health
(with Ahlea Khadro and Heather Dane)
Meditations to Heal Your Life
(also available in a gift edition)
Modern-Day Miracles (Louise & Friends)
The Power Is Within You
Power Thoughts
The Present Moment
The Times of Our Lives (Louise & Friends)
You Can Create an Exceptional Life
(with Cheryl Richardson)
You Can Heal Your Heart (with David Kessler)
You Can Heal Your Life (also available in a gift edition)
You Can Heal Your Life Affirmation Kit
You Can Heal Your Life Companion Book

You Can Heal Your Life (audio book)
You Can Heal Your Life Study Course
Your Thoughts Create Your Life

DVDs

Receiving Prosperity
You Can Heal Your Life Study Course
You Can Heal Your Life, The Movie
(also available in an expanded edition)
You Can Trust Your Life (with Cheryl Richardson)

CARD DECKS

Healthy Body Cards
I Can Do It® Cards
*I Can Do It® Cards . . . for Creativity, Forgiveness,
Health, Job Success, Wealth, Romance*
Power Thought Cards
Power Thoughts for Teens
Power Thought Sticky Cards
Wisdom Cards

CALENDAR

I Can Do It® Calendar (for each individual year)

and

THE ESSENTIAL LOUISE HAY COLLECTION
(comprising *You Can Heal Your Life, Heal Your Body,* and *The
Power Is Within You* in a single volume)

All of the above are available at your local bookstore, or may be
ordered by visiting: Hay House USA: www.hayhouse.com®
Hay House Australia: www.hayhouse.com.au
Hay House UK: www.hayhouse.co.uk
Hay House South Africa: www.hayhouse.co.za
Hay House India: www.hayhouse.co.in

Louise's websites: www.LouiseHay.com®
and www.HealYourLife.com®

Also by Robert Holden

<u>BOOKS</u>

Authentic Success (formerly titled *Success Intelligence*)
Be Happy
Happiness NOW!
Holy Shift!
Loveability
Shift Happens!

<u>CDs/DVDs</u>

Be Happy
Coaching Happiness
Follow Your Joy
Happiness NOW!
Loveability
Shift Happens!
Success Intelligence

<u>Flip Calendars</u>

Happiness NOW!
Success NOW!

All of the above are available at your local bookstore,
or may be ordered by visiting:
Hay House USA: www.hayhouse.com®
Hay House Australia: www.hayhouse.com.au
Hay House UK: www.hayhouse.co.uk
Hay House South Africa: www.hayhouse.co.za
Hay House India: www.hayhouse.co.in

Life
LOVES
You

7 Spiritual Practices to Heal Your Life

LOUISE HAY &
ROBERT HOLDEN

HAY HOUSE, INC.
Carlsbad, California • New York City
London • Sydney • Johannesburg
Vancouver • Hong Kong • New Delhi

Published and distributed in the United States by: Hay House, Inc.: www.hayhouse.com® • *Published and distributed in Australia by:* Hay House Australia Pty. Ltd.: www.hayhouse .com.au • *Published and distributed in the United Kingdom by:* Hay House UK, Ltd.: www .hayhouse.co.uk • *Published and distributed in the Republic of South Africa by:* Hay House SA (Pty), Ltd.: www.hayhouse.co.za • *Distributed in Canada by:* Raincoast Books: www.raincoast.com • *Published in India by:* Hay House Publishers India: www.hayhouse .co.in

Cover design: Leanne Sui Anastasi • *Interior design:* Jenny Richards

"Love After Love" from THE POETRY OF DEREK WALCOTT 1948-2013 by Derek Walcott, selected by Glyn Maxwell. Copyright © 2014 by Derek Walcott. Reprinted by permission of Farrar, Straus and Giroux, LLC. • Reprinted by permission of the translator: "Say Yes Quickly" by Jalal al-Din Rumi, *Open Secret*, trans. Coleman Barks, Boston: Shambhala Publications © 1984 by John Moyne and Coleman Barks. • "On Children" from THE PROPHET by Kahlil Gibran, copyright © 1923 by Kahlil Gibran and renewed 1951 by Administrators C.T.A. of Kahlil Gibran Estate and Mary G. Gibran. Used by permission of Alfred A. Knopf, an imprint of the Knopf Doubleday Publishing Group, a division of Random House LLC. All rights reserved. Any third party use of this material, outside of this publication, is prohibited. Interested parties must apply directly to Random House LLC for permission. • Excerpt from *The Parent's Tao Te Ching* by William Martin. Copyright © 03-31-1999 books-contributor-william-20martin. Reprinted by permission of da capo, a member of the Perseus Books Group. • "This Place Where You Are Right Now," from *The Subject Tonight Is Love*, © 2003. Used by permission of Daniel Ladinsky. • "So Many Gifts," from *The Gift: Poems by Hafiz, the Great Sufi Master*, © 1999. Used by permission of Daniel Ladinsky. • "The Sun Never Says," from *The Gift*, © 1999. Used by permission of Daniel Ladinsky. • "i thank You God for most this amazing". Copyright 1950, (c) 1978, 1991 by the Trustees for the E. E. Cummings Trust. Copyright (c) 1979 by George James Firmage, from COMPLETE POEMS: 1904-1962 by E. E. Cummings, edited by George J. Firmage. Used by permission of Liveright Publishing Corporation.

Library of Congress Cataloging-in-Publication Data of the original edition

Hay, Louise L.
  Life loves you : 7 spiritual practices to heal your life / Louise Hay, Robert Holden.
    pages cm
  ISBN 978-1-4019-4614-2 Hardcover
  1. Self-actualization (Psychology) 2. Affirmations. 3. Spiritual healing. I. Holden, Robert, 1965- II. Title.
  BF637.S4H3793 2015
  158--dc23   2014041154

Tradepaper ISBN: 978-1-4019-4616-6
10 9 8 7 6 5 4 3 2 1
1st edition, May 2015
2nd edition, April 2016

MIX
Paper from
responsible sources
FSC® C011935
www.fsc.org

Printed in the United States of America

Contents

Introduction

The first time I met Louise Hay in person was backstage at an I Can Do It! conference in Las Vegas. Reid Tracy, president of Hay House, introduced us. "Welcome to the Hay House family," Louise said, as she gave me a warm hug.

Louise was due on stage in ten minutes to welcome the crowd and introduce me as the first speaker of the day. "May I do your makeup for you?" she asked me. I don't wear makeup normally, but her offer was too good to turn down. Louise worked on my face with an array of brushes, powders, creams, and something glossy for my lips. We had great fun. Everyone backstage was highly amused. With her finishing touch, Louise looked me in the eyes and said, "Life loves you."

Life loves you is one of Louise's best-loved affirmations. I think of it as her signature affirmation, the heart thought that represents her life and her work. She loves to tell people, "Life loves you." Each time

I hear her say these words, I feel it like honey in my bones. Early on, I thought that *Life loves you* would be a great subject for a Louise Hay book. I mentioned it to Louise. I also spoke to Reid Tracy. "Tell me when you're ready to help her write it," he said. I didn't think he was serious. Anyway, I was busy with my own writing projects.

A few years passed, and I wrote three new books for Hay House: *Be Happy,* for which Louise wrote the foreword; *Loveability*; and *Holy Shift!* The idea of a book about *Life loves you* would pop into my mind occasionally, but I didn't do anything about it. The day after I finished *Holy Shift!,* I'd planned to play golf. However, by lunchtime I'd written a synopsis for *Life Loves You*, a book co-authored by Louise Hay and Robert Holden. I had no choice but to write the synopsis that morning. I didn't have to think about it. The words just tumbled onto the page.

I showed the synopsis to my wife, Hollie. "Where did this come from?" she asked me. I told her I was as surprised as she was. "Send it immediately," she said. I e-mailed Patty Gift, my editor, on October 7th. Later that day, Patty wrote that she and Reid Tracy loved my synopsis and that Reid would present it to Louise. Louise's birthday was October 8th. On October 9th, I got an e-mail from her, full of happy emoticons: balloons, cake, hearts, and gifts. She wrote, "I am so excited, Robert. How long have you been planning this, dear one? I am honored to be part of this special event. Life will help us in every way. Happy birthday to me! Much love, Lulu."

Our book, *Life Loves You*, is the fruit of a dialogue between Louise and me. I visited Louise in San Diego, California, three times between Thanksgiving and Easter. We spent a total of nine days together. I recorded all our conversations. We also scheduled regular calls on Skype. Over the years, Louise and I have met up at more than 20 I Can Do It! conferences in Europe, Australia, Canada, and America. I've interviewed Louise for the Hay House World Summit, and Louise has attended several of my public talks and workshops. As you will see, I share stories and conversations from some of these meetings as well.

Life Loves You is an inquiry that takes you to the heart of who you are. It explores your relationship with the world. It asks deep questions about the nature of reality. In recent years, science has learned to see the world in a new way. For instance, we know now that atoms are not separate little things but expressions of universal energy. A universe of separate things never really existed. Everything is part of everything. Each of us is part of a greater Unity. We have a relationship with the stars, with each other, with all of creation.

Science recognizes that the world is not just a physical place; it is also a state of mind. "The universe begins to look more like a great thought than like a great machine," wrote Sir James Jeans, the English physicist. Exploring the consciousness of creation is the new frontier of science. Louise and I believe that the basic building block of creation is not the atom; it is love. This love is not a sentimental thing. It is not just an emotion; it is the creative principle behind the dance of life. It is universal. It is intelligent. It is benevolent. We are all an expression of this love. It is our true nature.

Life Loves You is both an inquiry and a practical exercise. Louise is a spiritual pragmatist, and I am interested in philosophy only if it can be applied to everyday life. Hence we made the subtitle of our book *7 Spiritual Practices to Heal Your Life*. There are seven chapters, and each chapter ends with a spiritual practice that helps you turn theory into experience. In addition to the seven main practices, there are a number of other exercises, too. You might like to do the exercises in the book with a partner or in a study group. Please don't skip them. Love is not just an idea, after all.

In Chapter 1, Looking in the Mirror, we explore the Mirror Principle. This principle recognizes that our experience of the world mirrors our relationship with ourselves. *We see things not as they are but as we are.* Thus the world mirrors the basic truth about us, which is *I am loveable.* And it also mirrors our basic fear, *I am not loveable.* The world can be a dark and lonely place when we are estranged from our heart and do not love ourselves. However, one sincere act of self-love can help us experience creation's gentleness and see the world anew. The spiritual practice for Chapter 1 includes a practice called *Letting Life Love You* and a meditation, *Love's Prayer.*

In Chapter 2, Affirming Your Life, Louise and I talk about our school days and how we were first taught to see the world. I share a story about a lecture at college that changed my worldview forever. It was called "Do you honestly, truly, really believe that a flat tire can give you a headache?" Here we invite you to consider that life is not judging you, criticizing you, or condemning you. We suffer from our own psychology. Other people may hurt us too, but life itself is not against us. Why would it be? Life is deeply affirming. We are an expression of creation, and life wants us to be the Unconditioned Self we truly are. The spiritual practice for this chapter is called *10 Dots*.

Chapter 3, Following Your Joy, is about listening to your inner guidance. "*Life loves you* isn't about getting your own way; it's about getting out of your way," says Louise. Louise talks about her *inner ding*, and I talk about my *Yes* with a capital "Y." Life is always trying to guide us, support us, and inspire us. Sometimes we are too caught up in our own story and lost in our personal misery to be able to see this. The spiritual practice is to create an affirmation board, to help you follow your joy and live a life you love.

Chapter 4, Forgiving the Past, is the midpoint of our inquiry. Here we investigate some of the common blocks to letting life love you—for example the *fall from grace:* the perceived loss of innocence and source of our learned unworthiness. We explore the *guilt story*, a tale told by the superego that once upon a time life loved me and I was loveable, but not anymore. We talk about inner-child work and reclaiming our original innocence. The spiritual practice is called *The Forgiveness Scale*. It is one of the most powerful forgiveness exercises we know.

In Chapter 5, Being Grateful Now, Louise and I look at the principle of *basic trust* recognized by psychologists as essential in both childhood development and adult life. Basic trust is what we are born with. It's a *knowing*—we feel it in our bones—that we are part of creation and are supported by a loving and generous Unity. Basic trust recognizes that life doesn't just happen *to* you; it happens *for* you. It sees that you have the best seat in the house for your life. Every experience—good or bad, happy or sad, bitter or sweet—offers you an opportunity to let life love you. The spiritual practice for this chapter, *Daily Gratitude,* combines gratitude with mirror work.

Chapter 6, Learning to Receive, looks at the benevolent-universe theory from Buddhism. Louise shares her experience of painting a portrait of the Buddha called *The Blessing Buddha.* The painting took Louise five years to complete. Painting it was a profound meditation that helped her to feel more deeply the loving kindness that exists in the design of life. "Life is always trying to love us, but we need to be open if we are to see it," says Louise. The spiritual practice for this chapter is *A Receiving Journal.* The purpose of this journal is to help you recognize more clearly how life is loving you right now.

In Chapter 7, Healing the Future, we arrive at the question *Is the universe friendly?* Albert Einstein is said to have called this the most important question we can ask. Louise and I believe an equally important question is *How friendly am I?* At the deepest level, our purpose in life is to be a loving mirror to the world. Our goal is not just to let life love us but also to love life back. We are here to love the world. If each of us did this just a little bit more, the world would not be such a fearful place. The spiritual practice for Chapter 7 is called *Blessing the World.*

Louise and I are so happy that you hold our book in your hands. We are grateful for the opportunity to write it together. We hope and pray that our work supports you all the more in letting life love you and in being a loving presence in this world.

Life loves you!

Louise Hay and Robert Holden

CHAPTER 1

Looking in the Mirror

Love is a mirror,
it reflects only your essence,
if you have the courage to
look in its face.

RUMI

It's Thanksgiving Day.

Louise and I are enjoying a festive lunch with family and friends. We are seated together at one end of a large oval dining table that is laden with two huge turkeys, plates of organic vegetables, gluten-free breads, a Cabernet Franc wine, and a pumpkin pie with an almond crust. Heather Dane has lovingly prepared the food. She insists her husband, Joel, also deserves some credit. Chief Food Taster, perhaps. The conversation flows. Spirits are high. "Life loves you," says Louise as we raise our glasses in thanksgiving.

As the afternoon rolls on, Heather conjures up even more delights from her magical kitchen. The oval dining table is continually being laid and re-laid. I imagine it is enjoying the feast as much as we are. At one point, one of our party, Elliot, leaves the table and walks across the room to a full-length mirror hanging on the wall. Elliot stands still in front of the mirror. He then leans forward and kisses the mirror. Louise and I catch the moment and smile at each other.

After a little while, Elliot again excuses himself from the table. He walks back to the mirror. He kisses the mirror again. He returns to the table. He is very happy. Pretty soon, Elliot is making regular visits to the mirror. He's unaware that any of us are watching him. Yet by now we all are. And we are enchanted. You see, Elliot is only 18 months old. What he is doing is natural and playful. Children kiss mirrors.

When Elliot sees he has an audience, he beckons his father, Greg, to join him. Greg is reluctant to leave the table, but Elliot keeps motioning to him, using a mix of sign language and words. Greg can't resist his son's overtures. Soon enough, Greg is sitting in front of the mirror. Elliot kisses the mirror first and then waits for Greg to take his turn. Greg steadies himself. He leans forward and plants a kiss on the mirror. Elliot claps his hands and shrieks with delight.

"Louise, do you remember kissing yourself in the mirror as a young girl?" I ask.

"No, but I am sure I did," she says.

Louise then asks if I remember kissing the mirror as a young boy.

"No, I don't," I reply.

"We were all like Elliot once," Louise says.

"I'm sure that's true," I say.

"Yes, and we can all be that way again," she says.

"How so?" I ask her.

"By doing mirror work," says Louise, as if the answer is obvious.

"Why mirror work?"

"Mirror work helps you to love yourself again," she explains.

"Like we each did in the beginning?"

"Yes. And when you love yourself, you see that life loves you, too," she adds.

Kissing the Mirror

It's a bright spring day, and my son, Christopher, and I are home alone. My wife, Hollie, and daughter, Bo, are out enjoying some "girl time" at the Pottery Café, near Kew Gardens. Bo has just turned four years old, and she expresses her creativity beautifully and with such fun. They'll be home soon, and I look forward to seeing Bo's latest work. Knowing my daughter, it will be a rainbow plate, a wobbly cup with hearts, or a baby rabbit salt pot painted pink—the sort of thing that would not be out of place on the big old table at the Mad Hatter's tea party in *Alice's Adventures in Wonderland*.

Christopher is nearly six months old now. I feel like I've known him my whole life. Sometimes when our eyes meet, the roles we are playing disappear. I stop being a dad and he stops being a baby, and it's like we are two *soul friends* hanging out. I've had exactly the same experience with Bo many times. I can't imagine life without them, and it feels like we were always meant to be together. Louise believes that we choose the family that can give us the lessons and gifts we most need for our life journey. In her book *You Can Heal Your Life*, she writes,

I believe we are all on an endless journey through eternity. We come to this planet to learn particular lessons that are necessary for our spiritual evolution. We choose our sex, our color, our country; and then we look around for the perfect set of parents who will "mirror" our patterns.

Hollie and Bo call to say that they are on their way home and they have gifts for Christopher and me. I put the phone down, and I notice that Christopher is smiling. Christopher smiles a lot. Most babies do. It's in their nature. However, when Christopher gets into one of his smiling moods he can't stop himself. He ends up smiling at *everything*, even inanimate objects like an empty flower vase, a vacuum cleaner, or a screwdriver. I gather up Christopher in my arms and take him over to the mirror that sits over our fireplace.

"Dear Christopher, it is my great pleasure to introduce you to Christopher," I say, pointing to his reflection in the mirror. Christopher stops smiling. I'm caught by surprise. I thought he'd be full of smiles when he saw himself in the mirror. After all, he smiles at everything else. I introduce Christopher to his reflection again. And, once again, Christopher doesn't smile. In fact, his face has barely any expression on it. It's as if he hasn't seen anything. Not even an empty flower vase.

Why didn't Christopher smile at his reflection? Well, I did some research on the psychology of childhood development, and I discovered that it's common for young babies *not* to smile at themselves in the mirror. They don't recognize themselves. Why is this? I asked Louise about it. "Young babies are not identified with their body yet," she said in the matter-of-fact way that is so characteristic of her.

Young babies are like soul birds that fly over their body and have yet to land in them. When they look in the mirror, they don't point at the body and think, *That is me,* or *This is mine.* Babies are just pure consciousness. There is no thought of *I.* They have no self-image. They have not made a persona or mask. They do not experience neurosis as yet. They are still full of the original blessing of spirit. They are identified only with their *original face*, as Buddhists call it, which is the face of the soul.

Children commonly begin to identify with the image in the mirror between 15 and 18 months of age. This is the Mirror Stage, or *stade du miroir*, as the psychoanalyst Jacques Lacan called it. No wonder Elliot was having such a good time at our Thanksgiving feast. Sure enough, when Christopher reached Elliot's age, he started to kiss the mirror, too. He'd also kiss the big round bath tap in our family bath, shiny spoons, steel saucepans, glass doorknobs, and anything else that caught his reflection.

From about three years old, the mirror becomes a friend. Children love what they see in the mirror. This is the time when they learn *I have a body*. They still wear their body lightly, though. The body is not who they are, but it is a necessary form for the human experience. This is a time to try on faces, to pull poses, to play peekaboo, and to invent silly dances. Christopher and Bo are highly amused by the image they see in the mirror. They often play games with their image, just as Peter Pan plays with his shadow.

Experimenting with being a *me* is fun at first but not forever. As we take on the identity of a separate self—an ego—there is a shift in our psychology. We become self-conscious in front of the mirror. We are camera shy. We either crave attention or we avoid it. We take a detour out of love and into fear. We start judging ourselves, and we lose sight of our *original face*. The self-image that appears in the mirror is made up of judgments. It is not the real you.

The soul bird, which is our true nature, still sings, but it is difficult to hear her song above the raucous shrieks of a self-image, or ego, that feels separate and afraid. The beauty we once saw in the mirror is still with us, but it is distorted by our self-judgment. We can see it again the instant we stop judging, but judging is now a habit we are identified with. We have convinced ourselves that judging is seeing, but the opposite is true. You can see only when you stop judging.

Myth of Inadequacy

"My first suicide attempt was at nine years old," Louise tells me.

"What happened?" I ask.

"Well, obviously it didn't work," she says.

"The world would never have met Louise Hay if it had," I tell her.

"That's true," Louise replies with a smile.

"So, what happened?"

"I was told never to eat certain berries on the hillside because they were poisonous and I'd die. So one day, when things were too bad, I ate the berries and lay down to die."

Louise and I are sitting in front of a full-length mirror in her office at her home in San Diego. We are sharing our childhood stories. It is Louise's idea that we do this in front of the mirror. She looks directly into the mirror as she speaks. She maintains a steady eye contact with her reflection. I am struck by how honest and vulnerable she allows herself to be. She speaks with a soft and kind voice as she recounts her childhood. Her words still carry some sadness. She is full of compassion for her nine-year-old self.

"Why did you want to kill yourself?" I ask.

"I didn't feel loveable," she says.

"Did you ever feel loveable?" I ask.

"Yes, in the beginning. But everything hit the fan after my parents divorced. My mother remarried, to a man who abused me physically and sexually. There was a lot of violence in our home."

"I am so sorry to hear that, Lulu," I tell her.

"The family message was *I am not loveable*," she says.

When Louise was a teenager, a neighbor raped her. The man was sentenced to 16 years in jail. Louise left home at 15 years old. "All I wanted was for people to be kind," she says, "but I had no idea how to be kind to me." Things went from bad to worse. "I was starved for love, and I was a magnet for abuse," Louise tells me. She went to bed with anyone who was nice to her. Soon she was pregnant. "I couldn't take care of a baby, because I couldn't take care of me," she says.

When it's my turn for my childhood story, Louise begins by asking me, "What is it you most wanted when you were a child?" I look deep into my reflection in the mirror. My mind is blank at first. Soon the memories return. "I wanted to be seen," I tell her. She asks what I mean by that. "I felt like I wanted someone to tell me who I am and why I am here and that everything will be okay," I explain. As a child, I was full of wonder, and full of those big questions like *Who am I?* and *What is real?* and *Why do I have a life?*

When I was little, we moved from house to house. Mum wanted to be far away from her parents. Dad was always busy chasing work. Somehow we ended up back in Winchester, England, not far from Mum's family home. We rented a little house called Honeysuckle Cottage, and I have a lot of happy memories from that time. Later, when I was nine years old, we moved to a village called Littleton, into a house named Shadows. I remember thinking that it was a strange name for a home.

"Did your parents love you?" Louise asks.

"Yes, most definitely, but it was complicated."

"What happened?" she asks.

"My mum suffered from depression that would come and go, and come back again. The depression always arrived unannounced. Sometimes it would settle in for weeks. Mum just lay in bed, and we'd pray for the medication to kick in. Other times she was admitted to different mental hospitals, but she always tried to kill herself in those places."

"What about your dad?" Louise asks.

"He had his own demons," I tell her.

When I was about 15 years old, we found out that Dad had a drinking problem. He promised to stop. He stopped many times. He eventually left home and spent much of the last ten years of his life homeless, traveling from one temporary shelter to the next. It was a nightmare to live with two parents who were in such pain. The Holden family loved each other as best they could, but none us felt loveable inside. Not one of us could say, "I am loveable" and really mean it.

> *The reality of your being is that you are loveable.*
>
> LOUISE HAY, *HEART THOUGHTS*

Louise and I share a philosophy about the basic nature of people. We both know that the basic truth about everyone, including you, is *I am loveable.* Love is much more than just a feeling, an emotion. Love is your true nature. It is your spiritual DNA. It is the song of your heart. It is the consciousness of your soul. If we're fortunate, as children this basic truth—I am loveable—is mirrored by our parents, our school, our church, and our friendships and other relationships.

Mirroring is an essential part of childhood. Its highest purpose is to affirm the basic truth that *I am loveable.* It is through affirmative mirroring that we experience our eternal loveliness. We trust who we are, and we grow up to be mature adults who are a loving presence in the world.

The basic truth *I am loveable* has an opposite, the basic fear *I am not loveable.* The fear of not being loveable is reinforced by unhealthy mirroring in childhood. In our conversation in front of the mirror, Louise tells me, "I was raised by two people who didn't feel loveable. They weren't able to teach me that I am loveable because they did not know it themselves." Parents have to know about the basic truth of their own nature if they are to help their children love themselves.

The basic fear *I am not loveable* is not true; it's just a story. It feels true only because we identify with it. This stops us from enjoying our own company. We move away from ourselves. We forget about the soul bird that is our true nature. And the world becomes a symbol of our fear. We are scared to look in the mirror. "I speed up past mirrors," actor Bill Nighy once said. Fear of unloveability infects our psychology, which becomes full of self-judgment: *There's something wrong with me; I am bad; I am nothing.*

The basic fear coupled with the habit of self-judging cause us to experience something I call *the myth of inadequacy*. The myth of inadequacy expresses itself in self-talk like:

> I am not good enough.

> I am not smart enough.

> I am not successful enough.

> I am not beautiful enough.

> I am not strong enough.

> I am not interesting enough.

I am not creative enough.

I am not rich enough.

I am not thin enough.

I am not significant enough.

"This fear of being not enough has been present in everyone I've worked with," says Louise. The myth of inadequacy has nothing to do with the soul bird, our true nature. It is a learned unworthiness. It belongs to a temporary self-image that we act out until it becomes too painful to maintain. At some point we fall to our knees and say, "I want to heal my life," and "There must be another way." We outgrow the myth of inadequacy when we are willing to embrace again the basic truth *I am loveable.*

The Mirror Principle

"The first time I did mirror work was not easy," Louise tells me.

"What happened?" I ask.

"I looked for flaws. And I found plenty of them!" she says with a smile.

"Such as?"

"Oh, my eyebrows weren't right. I had too many wrinkles. My lips weren't the right shape. There was a long list."

"That must have been hard."

"I was very hard on myself at that point in my life," says Louise.

My first experience with mirror work was similar to Louise's. When I looked in the mirror, I came face-to-face with a crowd of judgments. Some of the judgments were about my appearance. I remember I didn't like my smile. I wanted it to be different—better somehow. *I'm not photogenic,* I told myself. The other judgments were even more personal and condemning— typical myth-of-inadequacy stuff like *I'm not successful enough; I'm not talented enough; I haven't done enough with my life; I'm not good enough and I never will be.*

"Were you tempted to stop doing the mirror work?" I ask Louise.

"Yes, but I had a good teacher who I trusted, and he helped me to feel safe in front of the mirror."

"How did he do that?"

"Well, he pointed out to me that the mirror wasn't judging me; it was me who was judging me. Therefore, I didn't need to be afraid of the mirror."

"That's the key to mirror work," I say.

"Yes," agrees Louise. "And he also showed me that when I looked in the mirror, I was only judging my appearance. I wasn't really looking at me."

"So, you stuck with the mirror work."

"Yes, and after a while I began to notice the little miracles," says Louise.

"Little miracles?"

"Green lights and parking spots!" she says with a big laugh.

"What do you mean?"

"Well, traffic lights seemed to turn green just for me. And good parking spaces would appear in places that were normally impossible. I was in the rhythm of life. I was easier on myself, and life was getting easier."

I, too, have a good teacher for mirror work. Her name is Louise Hay! Louise is regarded as a pioneer in mirror work and has been teaching the world about it for more than 40 years now. *Mirror work* is the name Louise uses for a series of exercises that you do in front of a mirror. These exercises include meditations, affirmations, and inquiries that are featured in her Heal Your Life program. I use mirror work with students of my work with The Happiness Project and in my three-day program called *Loveability*.

The Mirror Principle is the name I give to the main concept behind mirror work. It is the key to understanding why mirror work is so transformative and healing. The Mirror Principle also gives you the motivation to keep doing mirror work when you experience resistance. The Mirror Principle teaches that *your relationship with yourself is mirrored in your relationship with everyone and everything.*

Your relationship with yourself is, therefore, reflected in your relationship with family and friends, lovers and strangers, authority figures and rivals, heroes and villains. The Mirror Principle can help you track your relationship with yourself in all areas of your life. Your relationship with yourself is mirrored, for instance, in your relationship with:

> *time:* making time for what's important;
>
> *space:* enjoying the gifts of solitude;
>
> *success:* listening to your heart;

happiness: following your joy;

health: caring for your body;

creativity: how self-critical you are;

guidance: trusting your inner wisdom;

abundance: how present you are;

love: how undefended you are;

spirituality: how open you are.

The Mirror Principle shows you how you suffer and how you can heal, and how you block yourself and how you can set yourself free. It's the key to self-love and also to letting life love you. Recognizing how the Mirror Principle operates gives you the necessary awareness to make good choices in your relationships, your work, and your life in general. So before we go any further, let's take a closer look at the Mirror Principle:

Psychology is a mirror. Your psychology is a mirror of your self-image. Your sense of who you are influences the thoughts you most identify with. In other words, you think like the person you see in the mirror. "I used to think I was a victim of the world," says Louise, "so my psychology was full of fear and cynicism and defensiveness. Life was trying to love me, but I couldn't trust that. And I couldn't see it was because I didn't believe it." The most effective way to change your psychology is to change your mind about yourself first.

The world is a mirror. Perception is subjective, not objective. The brain receives more than 10 to 11 billion bits of information every second, according to some estimates. It would blow a fuse if it tried to process all of that. Instead, it filters the information and presents us with about 2,000 bits of information every second. Your self-image is the filter. What you see is what you identify with. *We see things not as they are, but as we are.* And that is how we relate to the world as hell or heaven, a trial or a gift, a prison or a classroom, a battlefield or a garden, a workhouse or a playground, a nightmare or a theater.

Relationships are a mirror. When we meet each other, we also meet ourselves. We discover that we are different in some ways but the same in most ways. What you bring to a relationship is what you experience. And what you withhold may be what is missing. Sometimes we extend the basic truth *I am loveable* to each other, and other times we project the basic fear *I am not loveable.* The less you love yourself, the harder you make it for others to love you. The more you love yourself, the more you recognize how loved you are.

Life is a mirror. "When we grow up we have a tendency to recreate the emotional environment of our early home life," wrote Louise in her *Love Yourself, Heal Your Life Workbook.* "We also tend to recreate in our personal relationships those we had with our mother and father." Your life is an expression of who you think you are. It mirrors your values, your ethics, and your choices. It shows you your thoughts. It reflects what you believe you deserve or don't deserve, who you blame, and what you take responsibility for.

The Mirror Principle gives you the key to experiencing "little miracles" in your life. The principle is summed up beautifully in *A Course in Miracles:* "Perception is a mirror, not a fact. And what I look on is my state of mind, reflected outward." The text goes on to say,

Projection makes perception.
The world you see is what you gave it,
nothing more than that.
But though it is no more than that, it is not less.
Therefore, to you it is important.
It is the witness to your state of mind,
the outside picture of an inward condition.
As a man thinketh, so does he perceive.
Therefore, seek not to change the
world, but choose to change your
mind about the world.

Miracle of Self-Love

> *In my room I have a mirror, and I call*
> *it my Magic Mirror. Inside this mirror*
> *is my very best friend.*
>
> LOUISE HAY, *ADVENTURES OF LULU*

"Mirror work wasn't easy for me in the beginning,"
Louise tells a roomful of students at my five-day seminar *Coaching Happiness*. "The most difficult words for

me to say were *I love you, Louise.* I shed a lot of tears, and it took a lot of practice. I had to breathe through my resistance each time I said *I love you* to myself. But I stuck with it. And I'm glad I did, because mirror work has transformed my life."

There are 150 people at the seminar, and they're hanging on Louise's every word. Among the students are many psychologists, therapists, and coaches who use mirror work both personally and professionally. Louise attended the seminar as a student for her own learning. However, when we came to the module on mirror work, I couldn't pass up the opportunity to ask Louise to talk to us, and fortunately for us, she was happy to do so.

Louise tells us about an early breakthrough she had with mirror work. "One day, I decided to try a little exercise," she says. "I looked in the mirror and said to myself, 'I am beautiful and everybody loves me.' Of course, I didn't believe it at first, but I was patient with myself, and it soon felt easier. Then, for the rest of the day, I said to myself wherever I went, 'I am beautiful and everybody loves me.' This put a smile on my face. It was amazing how people reacted to me. Everyone was so kind. That day I experienced a miracle—a miracle of self-love."

Louise is on a roll, and so I take this opportunity to ask her about the purpose of mirror work. Our conversation was recorded. Here's what Louise said:

> The real purpose of mirror work is to stop judging yourself and see who you really are. When you stick at mirror work, you get to see beautiful *YOU* in full awareness, without judging, criticizing, or comparing. You get to say, "Hi, kid, I'm with you today." And you become a true friend to yourself.

Louise's response reminds me of the old Sufi practice called *Kissing the Friend.* The Friend is spelled with a capital *F* because it refers to your Unconditioned Self—to the soul bird that is made of love and that loves you very much. In the practice of *Kissing the Friend* you take your ego—your self-image—to the Friend and let yourself experience the basic truth *I am loveable.* This meeting washes away all misperceptions about who you are. It helps you to let go of judging, criticizing, and comparing.

When I teach the Mirror Principle I share a poem called "Love after Love," by Derek Walcott. It's a beautiful poem about self-love that identifies the drama that exists between the basic truth of the Unconditioned Self (*I am loveable*) and the basic fear of the ego (*I am not loveable*). Walcott describes the Unconditioned Self as "the stranger who was your self" and "who knows you by heart" and "who has loved you / all your life." He encourages us to let our Unconditioned Self befriend our ego, which is full of fear and judgment. "Peel your own image from the mirror," he writes. "Sit. Feast on your life."

Louise agrees to answer questions from the group. The first question is about common mistakes people make doing mirror work. "Not doing mirror work is the biggest mistake!" Louise says. "Too many people don't do mirror work because they think it won't work before they've tried it." Once people start, they are often put off by the self-judging they witness, she says. "The flaws you see are not the truth of your being," Louise explains. "When you judge, you see flaws. When you love, you see your essence."

The next question is about common blocks to doing mirror work. "Mirror work doesn't work in theory; it only works in practice," Louise says. In other words, the key to mirror work is to do it and to be consistent about it. When Louise is asked if she still has days when she finds it difficult to look in the mirror, she replies, "Yes, and on those days I make sure I stay in front of the mirror until I feel better." She doesn't go out the front door until she feels in a more loving space, she tells us. After all, the world mirrors how we feel about ourselves.

Louise and I wrap up our session together with one more question. This time I ask her what has been the greatest gift of doing mirror work. She shares how mirror work taught her to love herself and how it accelerated her healing process when she had vaginal cancer nearly 40 years ago. "Love is the miracle cure," she says, "And when you are willing to love yourself more, every area of your life works out better." On that note, Louise takes her leave, signing off in familiar fashion: "Remember, life loves you," she says.

PRACTICE 1:
LETTING LIFE LOVE YOU

*Love yourself as much
as you can, and all of life
will mirror this love back to you.*

LOUISE HAY, *YOU CAN HEAL YOUR LIFE*

Louise and I are out to dinner at Mr. A's, which is one of Louise's favorite local restaurants. We are enjoying excellent food, fine wine from Burgundy, and a panoramic view of San Diego. I have flown in from London for another round of conversations for writing this book. We are both excited and grateful to be working together. During the meal, I present Louise with a gift. It's a silver pocket mirror with the inscription *Life Loves You*. Louise smiles. She opens the case and looks into the mirror. "Hi, Lulu," she says aloud. "Always remember that life loves you and life wants the best for you. All is well." She pauses for a moment and then hands the mirror to me. "Your go, kiddo," she says with a twinkle in her eye.

The first spiritual practice Louise and I have created for you combines self-love and mirror work. This practice has two parts to it. It takes about 15 minutes to do it, and the benefits will last a lifetime. The one piece of equipment you need is a mirror. Any mirror will do. Make sure you give it a good polish before you begin. You are about to meet the most important person in your life. Remember, your relationship with this person (namely *you*) influences your relationship with everyone and everything.

Let's begin! Be sure you are sitting comfortably. Look into the mirror. Inhale deeply. Say to yourself, *Life loves you* (or, *Life loves me*), and then exhale. It's good to keep breathing! Repeat this ten times. Notice your response each time. Pay attention to the three languages of response: sensation (body messages), feelings (heart thoughts), and thoughts (mental commentary).

We recommend that you write down your responses in a journal. Louise and I did this in order to track our progress. Sensations may include tension around the heart, tightness in the face, softening around the eyes, and lightness of being. Feelings may include sadness and grief; hope and happiness. Thoughts may include commentary like *I can't do this,* and *This isn't working.* Please don't judge your responses. There are no right answers. And don't try to be positive; be honest.

Notice that the phrase *Life loves you* is only three words long. There are no other words. It's not *Life loves you because . . .* For example, *because I am a good person,* or *because I work hard,* or *because I just got a raise,* or *because my football team won.* Similarly, it's not *Life will love you if . . .* For example, *if I lose ten pounds,* or *if I heal this cancer,* or *if I find a girlfriend. Life loves you* is about unconditional love.

After you complete ten rounds of the affirmation *Life loves you,* we invite you to look in the mirror and say this affirmation to yourself: *I am willing to let life love me today.* Once again, notice your responses. And remember to breathe. Repeat this affirmation until you feel comfortable sensations in your body, light feelings in your heart, and a happy commentary in your thoughts. Willingness is the key. With willingness, all things are possible.

"Please encourage people to be very kind to themselves when they do this practice," Louise tells me as I write notes for this chapter. "I know that mirror work can be very confronting at first. It reveals your most basic fear and your most terrible self-judgments. But if you keep looking in the mirror, you will begin to see through those judgments and see who you really are." Louise goes on to say, "Your attitude to mirror work is the key to success. It's important to take it lightly and be playful. If it helps, I prefer that people stop calling it mirror *work* and instead call it mirror *play.*"

Louise and I want you to do this spiritual practice every day for seven consecutive days. And we want you to start today. Doing it tomorrow won't make it any easier than doing it today. "I know from my own experience that whatever excuse I have today,

I'll still have tomorrow," Louise tells me. Remember, mirror work doesn't work in theory; it works in practice. You don't have to like this exercise or agree with it; all we ask is that you do it. It will get easier. Any discomfort or resistance you experience will dissolve if you meet it with love and acceptance. If you like, you can do this exercise with the support of a trusted friend, therapist, or coach.

The real goal of this first spiritual practice is to help you align yourself consciously with the basic truth *I am loveable.* When you feel loveable, you experience a world that loves you. Remember, the world is a mirror. There is no real difference between saying to yourself *I love you* and *Life loves you.* It's all the same love. When you let life love you, you feel loveable; and when you feel loveable, you let life love you. Now you are ready to be who you really are.

Please note: This practice is not about making yourself loveable; you already *are* loveable. You are a holy expression of love *now.* It is not about making yourself worthy; you already *are* worthy. It is not about improving yourself; it is about accepting yourself. It is not about changing yourself; it is about changing your mind about yourself. And it is not about reinventing yourself; it is about being even more of the real you.

We close Chapter 1 with a prayer I wrote that I often share in my seminars. It's called Love's Prayer. We think it sums up the spirit of love and acceptance, which this chapter is about.

Beloved One,
You cannot judge yourself and know who you are.
The truth about you cannot be judged.
Put aside your judgments then,
for one sweet holy moment,
and let me show you
something wonderful.

See what it's like to be you
when you stop judging yourself.
What you judge is just an image.
After the last judgment,
you will know yourself again.

Love will appear in your own mirror.
To greet you as your friend.
For you are loveable.
And you are made
of love.

CHAPTER 2

Affirming Your Life

*What we are today comes from our thoughts of
yesterday, and our present thoughts build
our life of tomorrow.*

THE BUDDHA

My children, Bo and Christopher, love Louise
Hay, and I know she feels the same way
about them. It's interesting watching them
together. Louise doesn't dote. She doesn't do tickles.
She doesn't play games. She treats Bo, who is six years
old, not as a "big girl" or a "good girl" but as a real
girl. Christopher, who is three years old, is a real boy.

And Louise is no age at all. And that's that. It's all perfectly natural. The way they are together reminds me of Mary Poppins with Jane and Michael.

The first time Christopher met Louise, he ran right up to her and shouted, "Would you like to see my teeth?" Louise considered his proposal for a moment and said, "Yes, I would." Christopher then looked up and grinned. "Thank you," said Louise. "That's okay," said Christopher. He hadn't done that with anyone before and hasn't repeated it since. Later on, I asked Louise about the significance of teeth. In her matter-of-fact way, she said, "Teeth are about making good decisions. He was simply telling me that he knows his own mind and that he is capable of making good decisions."

The first time we visited Louise's home, Louise gave Bo a tour. First she showed her the big, round dining table that she'd painted to resemble a swirling universe with galaxies and stars. "I'd like to paint our kitchen table, Dad," Bo told me. Louise then showed her an oil painting of a hippopotamus that she was working on. It's called "Oswald Doing the Rhumba." "Oswald is a happy hippo," Louise said. "He thinks happy thoughts because he knows that his mind is creative." In the garden, Louise showed Bo how to pull carrots and beetroots from the ground. They also picked kale and sugar snap peas. We now have a vegetable garden at home.

The first bracelet Bo made she gave to Louise. She chose the glass and ceramic beads herself and was most insistent that this was to be a present for Louise. From time to time, Louise sends me an e-mail saying, "Tell Bo I am wearing her bracelet today." One of my favorite e-mails from Louise was sent a few days after a family visit. She wrote, "Tell Christopher I still have his little handprint on my bedroom window. I'll wash it off one day. But not yet."

Back home in London, one of our breakfast rituals is sharing the daily affirmation from Louise's *I Can Do It* calendar. Bo loves to read stories first thing in the morning and just before bedtime. Two books in her collection are children's books written by Louise Hay. One is *I Think, I Am!*, which teaches kids about the power of affirmations. The other is *The Adventures of Lulu*, which is a collection of stories that help children to feel confident and be creative.

"Lulu is the girl I'd like to have been when I was growing up," says Louise. "She knows that she is loveable and that life loves her." Lulu and Bo are a similar age. They both have blond hair. Each has a little brother. Sometimes they get afraid. Sometimes they get hurt. And life teaches them how to listen to their heart and live with courage. There's a verse in one of Lulu's songs that says,

> You can be what you want to be,
> you can do what you want to do,
> you can be what you want to be,
> all of life supports you.

Bo and I were talking about Louise one day, and Bo was asking a lot of questions. "Why do you like Louise Hay so much?" I asked her. Bo thought for a moment, then smiled and said, "I like the way she thinks."

Your Radiant Intelligence

"I was a high school dropout," says Louise. "I was told I wasn't very smart, and that's what I told myself, too."

"How would you describe your experience of school?" I ask her.

"Terrible. I was very self-conscious, I didn't feel safe, and I had no friends."

"Why not?"

"My parents struggled for money. I wore hand-me-down clothes. I had an awful haircut that my stepfather gave me. I had to eat raw garlic to keep the worms away, which also kept all the children away."

"How did you get on with your teachers?"

"My teachers were on a different wavelength from me," Louise says.

What is the purpose of school? My education was a bewildering experience. I remember scary old teachers, dreaded algebra lessons, corporal punishment, short playtimes, and for lunch, always blancmange. What is blancmange anyway? Is it even a real food? My school report said that I was a polite boy who had a lot of potential. Potential for what? I never found out. I remember being scolded one day for not being original. "Holden, be original!" the teacher shouted. This really hurt me.

"I couldn't wait to leave school," says Louise firmly.

"You surprise me," I tell her. "You're my role model as a lifelong learner who is always open to learning new things."

"I didn't understand why I had to learn about battle dates, the Industrial Revolution, and the history of politics," she tells me.

"How did you get on with exams?" I ask.

"I failed most of them," Louise says.

A syllabus without a soul: That's how I describe my education. The curriculum was based on a narrow definition of intelligence. It was an intellectual exercise. We focused on "head" intelligence. We studied logic and literacy. We memorized and recited facts and figures. Little attention was given to the intelligence of the heart and to finding your inner voice. Like Louise, I wasn't very academic. My education showed all my weaknesses and none of my strengths.

"What a distressing contrast there is between the radiant intelligence of a child and the feeble mentality of the average adult," observed Sigmund Freud. We are each created with a radiant intelligence. It's in our spiritual DNA to want to learn and grow. Psychology studies show that young children, from about three years old, ask as many as 390 questions a day. Any parent can verify these findings. Children are blessed with a love of learning, and it is either nurtured or knocked out of them.

Girls and boys need a fairy godmother to help nurture their love of learning. A fairy godmother might be a loving parent, a wonderful schoolteacher, or an eccentric aunt, perhaps. Or maybe the fairy godmother takes the form of a musical instrument, a pony, or some other great passion. "I loved to draw and paint when I was young, and I always kept my desk neat and tidy," recalls Louise. "I also spent hours and hours reading. I especially liked fairy tales. My imagination was a safe and wonderful place to be."

I rediscovered my love of learning when I entered higher education to study psychology and philosophy. I went from being a C student at school to an A student who passed exams with distinction. How did this happen? The difference was that I could choose my subjects now. At last, I was learning about something that interested me. My learning wasn't just for a career or a future income. I was following a passion. And I was finding my voice.

Dwelling in Possibility

Louise and I are having dinner at her place. We are sitting at the big, round table with its swirling universe full of galaxies and stars. We are talking about how the world is not as physical as it looks but is really a state of mind. I have pen in hand, and we're drawing up a syllabus with a soul—a list of classes we wish we'd been taught as children. So far, the list includes classes on self-acceptance, love, meditation, nutrition, real happiness, forgiveness, and imagination.

"Imagine you could teach one class to every child on this planet; what would it be?" I ask. "How wonderful!" Louise says. She gives herself a moment to play with some possibilities. Sensing her readiness, I ask her what she'd call her class. "I'd teach a class on 'Making Friends with Your Mind,'" she tells me with a big smile.

"And how would you begin?" I ask.

"With mirror work, of course," she replies, in her matter-of-fact way. "And all the teachers and parents would have to attend, too."

"What would you teach in your class?" I ask.

"We'd start by looking in the mirror and affirming *Life loves you.*"

"*Life loves you,*" I repeat, letting the affirmation sink in.

"Then we'd say to our mirror, *I love you, I really love you,*" she says.

"I love you, I really love you," I affirm.

"We'd also say, *My mind is very creative, and I choose to think loving and happy thoughts today,"* she says.

"That's beautiful," I tell her.

"When we love ourselves, we naturally think beautiful thoughts," she tells me.

Most of the thoughts we think are not our real thoughts. They are primarily a gaggle of judgments, criticisms, doubts, and other commentary we have picked up along the way. These so-called thoughts come not from the original mind of our Unconditioned Self but from a self-image that believes the basic fear *I am not loveable.* This basic fear is not natural but learned. All our neuroses stem from it.

"Babies don't criticize themselves," Louise says. That's true. Imagine meeting a newborn baby that didn't like its wrinkles. Babies don't feel inadequate. They don't appear to judge themselves or others as being not good enough or not cute enough or not smart enough or not successful enough. Babies don't hold resentments. On the contrary, it's amazing to witness how quickly they dry their tears and how easily they let things go. Babies are not pessimistic. They haven't given up on the future. They are still with their original mind, and they dwell in possibility.

Your original mind reflects the basic truth *I am love-able*. It is a consciousness of love—a radiant intelligence empty of the psychology that reflects the basic fear *I am not loveable*. Michael Neill is an author Louise and I love and respect. Michael teaches people how to think. "At any moment you're either with your thoughts, or you're in love," he says. In other words, you're tuning in to either the psychology of your self-image or the pure awareness of your Unconditioned Self.

The totality of possibility is how Louise describes the consciousness of the Unconditioned Self. "It's a phrase I learned from one of my early teachers, Eric Pace," says Louise. "I met Eric at the Church of Religious Science in New York, when I was in my mid-40s. I'd recently been divorced. I was feeling unloveable and like life didn't love me. Eric taught me that if you change your thinking, you can change your life. Each time you drop a limitation—a judgment, a criticism, a fear, a doubt—you open yourself up to the totality of possibilities that exists in the infinite intelligence of your original mind."

So how do you experience your original mind? There's a beautiful inquiry I teach in my *Loveability* program. If you'd like to try it, all you need do is make a quiet space for yourself, just as you would for a basic meditation practice. Let your body relax, place a hand on your heart, and let your thoughts be still. Then ask yourself this question: *What is it like to be me when I am not judging myself?* Repeat this question once every minute for 15 minutes, and with practice you will surely experience the loving awareness of your original mind.

In a recent *Loveability* seminar, I taught this inquiry at the front of the room to a student named Amanda. Her first response to the question *What is it like to be me when I am not judging myself?* was "I'm not sure if I've ever experienced myself without judgment." That's how it can feel when we forget about the basic truth *I am loveable.* Eventually, Amanda found her flow. By the end of the inquiry, she was "in heaven," as she put it. In her feedback to the group, Amanda said, "I had no idea it could feel this good to be me."

I recommend that you follow up this inquiry with a simple exercise. The idea is to complete the following sentence five times: *One good thing that could happen if I judged myself less is . . .* Don't edit yourself or judge your answers. Allow your original mind to speak to you. Let yourself dwell in possibility. And let the basic truth of who you are inspire and guide you.

Suffering from Psychology

One of the best classes I ever took was in my first year at Birmingham City University. It was a talk on cognitive therapy given by a guest lecturer, Dr. Anderson. The title of the lecture had piqued everybody's interest: "Do you honestly, truly, really believe that a flat tire can give you a headache?" Physically, Dr. Anderson resembled the actor Dick Van Dyke. He was full of happiness, and we liked him from the start.

Dr. Anderson briefly outlined the history of cognitive psychology. He mentioned Aaron Beck and Albert Ellis, considered pioneers in the field, and talked about the recent rise of cognitive behavioral therapy. He was most insistent, though, that cognitive psychology was *not* a new science. "Allow me to introduce you to one of the original fathers of cognitive psychology," he said as he waved a small book at us. He told us that the book in his hand contained wisdom thousands of years old. "If I may, I'd like to read the first line of this mighty tome to you," he said, thumbing through the pages of the introduction.

Here's what Dr. Anderson read to us:

> What we are today comes from
> our thoughts of yesterday,
> and our present thoughts build our life of tomorrow:
> our life is the creation of our mind.

As he looked up from the page, Dr. Anderson spread his arms and reached out to us, like a symphony conductor receiving applause at the end of a concert. Joy was pouring out of him. His demeanor said, "Behold, I have given you the secret of creation." None of the students applauded, but Dr. Anderson certainly had our attention. The book he was reading from was *The Dhammapada*, a collection of verses spoken by the Buddha.

"Raise your hand," Dr. Anderson said, "if you honestly, truly, really believe that a flat tire can give you a headache." Every hand went up. "Wrong answer," he said emphatically. "Yes, it can," we protested. "How?" he asked. The only way a flat tire can cause a headache, he argued, is if the tire comes off the wheel, bounces against a tree, and rebounds onto your head. We conceded his point. "How annoying!" said one student, who didn't like how this was going. Dr. Anderson said, "Raise your hand if you honestly, truly, really believe that a lecture can annoy you."

How do you experience the world? This was the real question that Dr. Anderson was posing. If you could put a magnifying glass up to any experience you've ever had, you'd see that the experience was made up of a circumstance *and* your thoughts about the circumstance. Life is made up of events and also your thoughts about these events. "When I was diagnosed with cancer," says Louise, "what I first had to treat were my thoughts about the cancer. I had to heal my thoughts first so I could treat the cancer with courage, wisdom, and love."

It's your thoughts that count. How you experience your life is unique to you, because only you experience your thoughts. That's why any two people will handle a similar situation in different ways. Here's a good example. After a recent visit to see Louise in San Diego, I took a British Airways flight home to London. The flight encountered severe turbulence nonstop for 90 minutes. We all experienced the turbulence, but we didn't experience it the same way. One lady screamed over and over, "I don't want to die!" She had to be sedated. A few seats away, two young boys met each violent bump and drop with howls of laughter. They were having a great time. And then there was the Englishman who sat with his eyes closed, breathing deeply and affirming to himself, *Life loves us,* and *All is well.*

Thought is not reality. I do the school run with my daughter, Bo. It's a 30-minute trip, depending on traffic. Our journeys are full of conversation. Bo loves her school, but she finds the drop-off difficult. "I know it's just my thoughts, Daddy," she said one time. "Be kind to those thoughts, and let them know you're okay," I said. Bo was quiet for a while, and then she asked a question—one of approximately 390 questions per day—which was, "What is a thought made of?" What a great question. When we know that thoughts are just ideas—a version of reality, but not reality itself—it can make a world of difference how we experience life.

You can choose your thoughts. Louise and I were out for a walk one day. We were following a nature trail near her home. Big old eucalyptus trees shaded us from the bright sun. We got talking about the principle *You can choose your thoughts.* "What exactly does this principle mean?" I asked Louise. She said, "It means thoughts have no power other than what you give them." Thoughts are just ideas—possibilities in consciousness—that are only big or powerful if we identify with them. "You are the only thinker in your mind, and you can choose if your thoughts are true or not," said Louise.

One of my favorite Louise Hay principles is, *The only thing we are ever dealing with is a thought, and a thought can be changed.* Most of the time when we are in pain, it's because we are responding to our thoughts about something. The pain is mind-made. It is a sign that we are literally suffering from psychology. The way out of suffering is to make friends with your mind and remind yourself that you are the thinker of your thoughts. Happiness is only ever one thought away. For instance:

When your three-year-old son puts the car keys down the toilet again in order to see the look on your face, you could get angry, or you could choose a higher thought.

When your six-year-old daughter asks you to dress up in her mother's wedding dress, you could be sensible and say "No," or you could choose to create a wonderful photo opportunity.

When your wife puts your favorite 1989 Bordeaux wine in the spaghetti sauce, this could be grounds for a major grievance, or you could choose peace instead.

When your computer crashes in the middle of writing a chapter of a book, you could declare atheism as revenge, or you could ask for extra help and guidance.

When something doesn't go your way, you could think, *The world is against me,* or you could choose to look for a hidden blessing.

Power of Inquiry

I was writing an article for a national newspaper. It was not going well. The editor had given me a deadline of "a thousand words by yesterday, ideally." I had been at my computer for more than two hours, and I was still staring at a blank screen. I had written more than a thousand words already, but none of them were any good, according to the voice in my head. That voice, the one that didn't like my writing, was familiar to me. It had a harsh tone. It felt cold and sharp. It was my inner critic.

My inner critic was firmly in charge of my writing that morning. I had a good idea what I wanted to say, but I couldn't get past the first line. Whatever I wrote was being judged by my inner critic as *not good enough* or *not interesting enough* or *not original enough.* I tried to reset myself over and over again. Deep breath. Sip of coffee. Inspiring affirmation. No luck whatsoever. I had wasted half a morning, and I felt like tearing my hair out. I didn't though, because I've tried that before and it doesn't work. At least, it doesn't work for me.

I was about to let the curtain fall on my career as a writer when I had a flash of insight. Another voice inside my head spoke to me. This voice sounded soft, warm, and resonant. It was kind. This voice said to me, "Your inner critic has never been published." "What?" I gasped. "Could this really be true?" Apparently it was. My inner critic—the voice that was coaching me how not to write my article that morning—had not once been published.

For years, I had listened faithfully to the voice of my inner critic, and I had not once thought to check its credentials. I just assumed that it spoke the truth and knew what it was doing. But my inner critic had never written a book. It didn't even have a blog. No wonder it couldn't show me how to write. Wow! I felt a huge surge of relief move through my body. I knew I had to stay close to that other voice that had delivered this amazing insight. "What shall I do now?" I asked the kind voice. "Tell your inner critic to relax and take the day off," the voice said. That's what I did. And the writing flowed.

"Awareness is the first step to changing anything," says Louise. "Until you are aware of what you are doing to yourself, you will not be able to make the change." That morning, as I sat at my computer, I allowed myself a new awareness. I let myself see what I was doing to myself. That sudden flash of insight, which in emotional intelligence theory is called *the magic quarter-second*, was enough to halt a pattern of self-criticism that was as old as I was. The inner critic still has an opinion about my writing every so often, but now I know what to do, thanks to the new awareness.

The heart of my work is inquiry. I coach people on how to use self-inquiry to be more self-aware and, ultimately, happier. I firmly believe that most people don't need more therapy; they need more clarity. In other words, the essence of who you are—your Unconditioned Self—doesn't need fixing or healing, because you're not really broken. When you're in pain, it's because you're suffering from psychology. "Even self-hatred is only a thought, and it's a thought that can be changed," says Louise. Self-awareness gives you choices.

Who taught you how to think? I ask this question in my training programs. Most people have never thought about it. We don't really question our thinking. "Children learn by imitation," says Louise. It's true. You have been taught how to think. You have followed someone's example. Guess whose? Do you know? "Most of us make up our minds about ourselves and the world by the time we are five years old," says Louise. In her book *You Can Heal Your Life,* Louise wrote,

> If we were taught as a child that the world is a frightening place, then everything we hear that fits that belief we will accept as true for us. The same is true for "Don't trust strangers," "Don't go out at night," or "People cheat you."

> On the other hand, if we were taught early in life that the world is a safe place, then we would hold other beliefs. We could easily accept that love is everywhere, and people are so friendly, and I always have whatever I need.

Without self-awareness, which gives you the ability to question your thoughts, you can't update your mind. The worst-case scenario is that you are running around with a secondhand mind, borrowed from a parent or someone else, and you are still using an old operating system—Mind 5.0—that is the mind of your five-year-old self. What you are calling *my mind* is not really yours, and it's out of date. Until you see this, your life will be full of familiar patterns, and nothing will change, no matter how hard you try.

Another great inquiry practice is to ask, *Who is thinking "my" thoughts*? There are two levels to consider here. Level one is investigating whether the thoughts you observe are yours or someone else's. For example, is self-criticism a family pattern? Does your self-criticism mirror your mother's self-criticism or her criticism of you? Does the way you judge yourself mirror your father's self-judgments or how he judged you? Is your philosophy a mirror of your family ethos? It's good to know whose example you are following. It's also good to know that you can choose your thoughts.

Level two of *Who is thinking "my" thoughts?* brings you even closer to home. Here you are observing if the thought is a reflection of either a) the basic truth *I am loveable*, which mirrors the original mind of your Unconditioned Self, or b) the basic fear *I am not loveable*, which mirrors the psychology of your self-image. In other words, is this thought a soul-thought or an ego-thought?

Which "me" is thinking this thought? Let's look at some examples:

I don't know: When you say to yourself, *I don't know,* is that what you really mean, or are you trying to say, *I don't think I know*? There is a world of difference. "Every time you say 'I don't know,' you shut the door to your own inner wisdom," says Louise. "But when you say to yourself, 'I am willing to know,' you open yourself up to the wisdom and support of your higher self."

I'm not ready: When you hear yourself say, *I'm not ready,* is it your soul speaking or your ego? Lots of us encounter this thought before we start something new like getting married, having a baby, creating a business, writing a book, or giving a public talk. Is it really true you're not ready? If so, get some extra help. If not, tell your ego to relax and let your soul lead the way.

I'm too old: We spend our life thinking, *I'm not ready,* and then one day it changes. We stop thinking, *I'm not ready* and start thinking, *I'm too old.* Who says? How old is your soul anyway? Are you too old really, or do you feel unworthy or afraid or something else? When you watch your thoughts, and you suspend your judgments, you get to see what the real thought is.

I can't do it: "A thought is just an idea," Louise says. "And you are either thinking with the mind of your soul or the mind of your ego." One of my favorite chapters in Louise's book *You Can Heal Your Life* is entitled "Is It True?" If you haven't read that chapter, please do. If you have read it, read it again. Every unexamined fear is 100 percent true until you look at it.

PRACTICE 2:
10 Dots

Louise and I are having lunch together at Torrey Pines Lodge in La Jolla, a few miles north of San Diego. Our table looks out on the Torrey Pines golf course, which is one of the most beautiful municipal courses in the world. It hosted the U.S. Open in 2008. Louise knows how much I love the game of golf and how thrilled I am to be here. I tell her I'm going to suggest to Reid Tracy, president of Hay House, that the annual Hay House Golf Championship be played here this year. "Everything is possible," says Louise with a smile.

We have been talking all morning about how the mind influences our experience of the world. "Golf is definitely a mind game," I say to Louise. "Everything is," she replies. I tell her about a recent round of golf I played in a tournament at St. Enodoc, in Cornwall, England, where I am a member. Like Torrey Pines, this course is set on the coast, and when the wind blows, it can be very difficult to control your ball and control your mind.

In this round, I played with someone who shot 120, which for him is about 30 more than usual. His game started poorly and got worse as it went on. I watched as his inner critic took control. Eventually, he found it impossible to keep his self-talk to himself. Shot after shot he yelled, "I am so stupid," or something similar.

"That's an affirmation," Louise says. His mind was like a giant sand trap that he couldn't get out of. "If you don't know how to change your mind, you can't change your experience," Louise tells me, sounding like a true golf pro.

Later that afternoon, Louise and I continue our conversation about the ability to change our minds.

"I don't change anyone's life," says Louise. "Only you can change your own life."

"So what do you do?" I ask.

"I teach people that the mind is very creative, and that when you change the way you think, it will change your life."

"So you teach people how to think," I say.

"Until someone can show you the connection between your outer experiences and your inner thoughts, you will be a victim of life," she says.

"They will feel like the world is against them," I say.

"The world isn't against us, though," says Louise. "The truth is that we are all loveable and life loves us."

"This awareness opens us up to the totality of possibilities," I suggest.

"The totality of possibilities is always here for us," says Louise.

I tell Louise that her live lecture "The Totality of Possibilities" is one of my favorites. In it she says, "I spend my life seeing the truth in people. I see the absolute truth of their being. I know that the health of God is in them and can express itself through them." Louise isn't talking about positive thinking. In fact, I don't think I've ever heard Louise use the term *positive thinking*. Louise doesn't see thoughts as being positive or negative. Thoughts are always neutral. It's the way we handle our thoughts that is either positive or negative.

"So how do we really change our mind?" I ask Louise.

"You have to change your relationship to your mind," she says.

"How do we do that?"

"By remembering that you are the thinker of your thoughts."

"Be the thinker, not the thought," I say.

"The power is with the thinker, not the thought," she responds.

"Notice the judgment, but don't be the judge,"

I say. "Notice a self-criticism, but don't be your own worst critic."

I remind Louise of my golf story and my golf partner's self-talk. He didn't yell, "What a stupid shot!" He yelled, "I am so stupid!" His self-talk wasn't a commentary on his golf game; it was about him. He got lost in his thoughts. He was so identified with each judgment that he was acting as the judge. It was the same with his self-criticism. He had become his own worst critic. He was no longer in his right mind. He probably didn't realize that his inner critic had never won a golf tournament.

"Your thoughts mirror your relationship with yourself," Louise reminds me.

"And a thought can be changed," I say.

"Yes, because you are the thinker of your thoughts," she says.

"How do we begin to change our thoughts?" I ask.

"Affirmations in front of the mirror," says Louise, as if it's obvious.

"What exactly is an affirmation?" I ask her.

"An affirmation is a new beginning," she replies.

Louise transformed her life by using affirmations. "I learned that every thought you think and every word you say is an affirmation," she tells me. "They affirm what you believe to be true and, therefore, how you experience your life." A complaint is an affirmation. Gratitude is an affirmation. Every thought and every word affirms something. Decisions and actions are also affirmations. The clothes you choose to wear, the foods you choose to eat, and the exercise you choose to do or not do—they are affirming your life.

"The moment you say affirmations, you are stepping out of the victim role," writes Louise in her book *Heart Thoughts*. "You are no longer helpless. You are acknowledging your own power." Affirmations wake you up from the sleep of the daily unconscious. They help you choose your thoughts. They help you let go of old limiting beliefs. They help you to be more present. They help you to heal your future. "What you affirm today sets up a new experience of tomorrow," says Louise.

When you spend time with Louise, you get to see that Louise Hay doesn't just think about affirmations; she lives her affirmations. She doesn't just do ten minutes of affirmations in the morning and then get on with her day. She takes her affirmations with her all through the day. To help, she has affirmations discreetly placed around her home. Affirmations like *Life loves me* on her bathroom mirror; *All is well* by a light switch in the hall; and *Only good lies before me* on her kitchen wall. One in her car reads, *I bless and prosper everyone in my life, and everyone in my life blesses and prospers me.*

It's now time to introduce you to the second spiritual practice of *Life Loves You*. It's called *10 Dots*. The idea is to practice one affirmation throughout the day. We recommend you start with the affirmation that's the main theme of this book. We invite you to begin the day by looking in the mirror and saying out loud, *Life loves you.* Please repeat this ten times. For variation you may wish to affirm:

I am open to life loving me today.

I allow life to love me today.

I say YES to life loving me today.

I am grateful for life loving me.

Life loves me, and I feel blessed.

Next, we want you to place ten dots in places where you will see them throughout the day. You can find self-adhesive dots in most stationery stores. Any shape will do: a circle, a star, a heart, a little angel, a smiley face. Stick these dots on your mirrors, your teakettle, your refrigerator, your car steering wheel or dashboard, your wallet, your computer screen, and anywhere else you may frequently look. Every time you see one of your ten dots, be sure to affirm consciously *Life loves me*.

We encourage you to do the *10 Dots* experiment for seven days. "Be patient with yourself," says Louise. "It's not like I said three affirmations and then set up Hay House." It's common in the beginning to experience some resistance. Also, you may find that you experience the opposite of the affirmation—thoughts and feelings that reflect the belief *Life doesn't love me*. Remember, this affirmation is a new beginning. It is realigning your thinking with the basic truth *I am loveable*. It will most likely require a period of adjustment. Stick with it. Just as with mirror work, affirmations don't work in theory; they work in practice.

CHAPTER 3

Following Your Joy

If you want the truth, I'll tell you the truth.
Listen to the secret sound, the real sound,
which is inside you.

KABIR

L ouise and I are sitting in front of the mirror again, the one in her office at home in San Diego. Today we are exploring the meaning of *Life loves you*. "*Life loves you* is a beautiful affirmation," I say, "but it's more than just an affirmation." Louise gives me one of her knowing smiles. "I hope so," she says. *Life loves you* offers us a basic philosophy for living. These three words are a signpost that points us to the heart of creation, to our relatedness to each other, and to our true nature. *Life loves you* shows us who we are and how to live a truly blessed life.

"What does *Life loves you* mean to you, Louise?" I ask.

"Life loves us *all*. It doesn't just love you or me," she replies.

"So we are all included," I say.

"Life loves all of us," she repeats.

"Love must include us all, or else it is not love," I say.

"Yes, and no one is more special than anyone else," says Louise.

"We are all equals in the eyes of love," I say.

"Yes, and no one is left out," she says.

"No unholy exceptions!" I add.

This may be a new way of thinking to some people, but it is not a new philosophy. Since ancient times, philosophers and poets have observed a basic relatedness we all share. In "Love's Philosophy," the poet Percy Bysshe Shelley explores this basic relatedness in a way that is both spiritual and sensuous. It's one of my favorite love poems. I always recite it at the start of my *Loveability* program. It begins:

> The fountains mingle with the river
>   And the rivers with the ocean,
> The winds of heaven mix forever
>   With a sweet emotion;
> Nothing in the world is single;
>   All things by a law divine
> In one spirit meet and mingle.
>   Why not I with thine?

We are made for each other. All of us are included. No unholy exceptions. Mystics and scientists agree that in the deeper reality beyond space and time, we are all members of one body. Albert Einstein referred to the perception of separateness as an "optical delusion." David Bohm, an American quantum physicist who was one of Einstein's most famous students, recognized an undivided universe, an implicate wholeness, and a theater of interrelations. We belong to each other.

"Life loves you unconditionally," says Louise.

"What does that mean?" I ask.

"Life is not judging you," she replies most emphatically.

"And life is not criticizing you," I add.

"No, and life is not testing you. And it's not trying to make things hard for you," Louise says.

"When you say *you*, I assume you mean the soul bird, our Unconditioned Self."

"Yes, life loves you, the real you," she says.

"We are loved for who we are, not for what we think we must become," I say.

"Life loves you now!" Louise emphasizes.

Life loves you is stated in the present tense. It's not that life loves you only when you are a child, young and innocent. And it's not that life will love you when or if you change. "Life loves us even when we don't love ourselves," says Louise. We both pause to let this awareness sink in. *Life loves you* feels natural and believable "when" and "if" we love ourselves, but otherwise it seems too good to be true. A passage from *A Course in Miracles* pops into my head. I share it with Louise.

> The universe of love does not stop
>   because you do not see it,
> nor have your closed eyes lost the
>   ability to see.

Look upon the glory of His creation,
   and you will learn what
God has kept for you.

"Let's talk about the meaning of life," I say to Louise. "Okay then," she replies, giving me a quizzical look. I ask her what the word *life* refers to in *Life loves you*. She tells me that *life* refers to whatever created us. She says that *life* can mean Universe, or Spirit, or Grace, or the Divine, or God. I sense her reluctance to use the word God, and I ask about this. She tells me, "I like to use the word *life* because *life* isn't a religious word." I understand her reluctance. "What a shame we made a religion out of God," I say.

"*Life loves you* is a spiritual philosophy, not a religious philosophy," says Louise.

"Life is 100 percent nondenominational," I say.

"Yes," says Louise, "and *life* is bigger than all the names of God put together."

"So, is *Life loves you* the same as *God loves you*?" I ask her.

"Yes, but only if God is not a man in the sky watching your genitals, and only if God is unconditional love."

"Amen," I say.

Life loves you is a philosophy of love that recognizes love as being spiritual, not just romantic. Like other philosophies, such as mystical Christianity, Sufism, the Kabbalah, and Bhakti yoga, love is bigger than just an emotion or sex. The love in *Life loves you* refers to the Mind of Creation. Love is the consciousness of the universe. It is empty of personal neurosis and ego psychology. "Love is an infinite intelligence," says Louise. "It loves all of its creations, and it will guide you and direct you if you will let it."

"Let's look at what *Life loves you* doesn't mean," I say to Louise. She gives me another quizzical look. "Well, *Life loves you* isn't about getting your own way; it's about getting out of your way," she says with a smile. "Life has a plan for each of us. This plan is for our highest good and for the greatest good of everyone. It's a Universal Plan that is bigger than any ego gratification. It has our highest interests at heart. All we can ever do is let love lead the way."

"When did you first consider the possibility that life loves you?" I ask.

"Oh, not for the longest time," Louise replies.

"Did anyone ever say to you, 'Life loves you,' while you were growing up?"

"No, not anyone. Certainly not anyone in my family."

"Did you learn it from someone?" I ask her.

"Not that I remember," says Louise.

"So how did you discover that life loves you?"

"It must have been when I found my inner ding," she says.

Listen from Within

Louise and I are at Hay House headquarters in Carlsbad, California. We are about to be filmed for the Hay House World Summit 2014. The cameras are in position. The studio lights are on. Louise is applying some final touches of makeup to my brow. Yes, Louise Hay does my makeup. It's a tradition of ours. She first offered to do my makeup when we met backstage at the Las Vegas I Can Do It! conference. That was my debut keynote for Hay House, and Louise has been my makeup artist ever since.

"Let's talk about your inner ding," I say.

"Oh yes. Ding, ding," says Louise, who is in a playful mood.

"What is your inner ding?" I ask.

"Well, I feel it right here," she says, tapping her chest.

"In your heart," I say.

"Yes," she says.

"So, what is the inner ding?"

"It's an inner knowing," she says.

Louise trusts her inner ding with her life. "It's my friend," she tells me. "It's an inner voice that talks to me. I've learned to trust it. It's right for me." I've interviewed Louise about her inner ding on three occasions. Each time I am struck by how grateful she is for her inner ding. She talks about it with reverence and love. Listening to her inner ding is a daily spiritual practice. "My inner ding is always with me," she says. "When I listen to my inner ding, I find the answers I need."

"Where does your inner ding come from?" I ask.

"Everywhere!" says Louise, still being playful.

"What does that mean?" I ask.

"My inner ding is how I listen to the big wisdom," she says.

"Is this like the One Intelligence you refer to in *You Can Heal Your Life*?" I ask.

"Yes, the One Intelligence that offers guidance to us all," she says.

"Do we all have an inner ding?" I ask her.

"Every child is born with an inner ding," Louise assures me.

This was my cue to tell Louise a story. Earlier that day, Hollie, Bo, Christopher, and I had visited the San Diego Botanic Garden, in Encinitas. We walked through a dragon tree grove, climbed up to a tree house (several times), counted butterflies, played by a waterfall, and ran around a grass maze. On our way back to our car, I stopped to look at a bed of orange California poppies. Bo came and stood next to me. "Daddy," she said, "the thing about love is you've got to love plants as much as you love people, and when you can do that, you know what love is."

"That's Bo's inner ding!" says Louise, clapping her hands with joy. One moment Bo is being a girl, and the next, suddenly she's Tinker Bell, waving her wand, dispensing wisdom like fairy dust. Every parent can testify to his or her child's inner ding. Children are blessed with a radiant intelligence. Some Buddhists call it *mirror-like consciousness* because it mirrors the wisdom of the soul. This wisdom has nothing to do with IQ scores, math tables, history tests, or Pythagorean triangles. You don't learn it; you bring it with you.

We are infused with natural wisdom. Our being is the knowledge of the universe. We each experience it in our own way, and we may call it by another name, such as inner ding, inner teacher, Mister God, Holy Spirit, or divine guidance. We carry the truth within us. In Robert Browning's poem "Paracelsus" he writes,

> Truth is within ourselves, it takes no rise
> From outward things, whate'er you may believe.
> There is an inmost centre in us all,
> Where truth abides in fullness; and around
> Wall upon wall, the gross flesh hems it in,
> This perfect, clear perception—which is Truth.

Somehow we forget about this truth, but it does not forget about us. Early on, we experience a loss of guidance. The GPS of our soul is in perfect working order, but we act as if it is broken. We learn to depend on the ego and our intellect for navigation. This is good for short journeys, but not for the journey that is our true path. Much of our life is spent trying to recover our inner wisdom—the inner ding. We have a memory of it, and this spurs us on.

"How did you find your inner ding again?" I ask Louise.

"I was a late bloomer," she says. "I'd bumbled along all through my adult life without any awareness of my inner ding."

"So what happened?"

"Well, I was sitting in a lecture at the Church of Religious Science in New York, and I heard someone say, 'If you are willing to change your thinking, you can change your life.' Something inside me said, 'Pay attention to this,' and I did."

"Was it your inner ding that said, 'Pay attention'?" I ask.

"It must have been," says Louise.

Louise then asks me how I found my inner ding. I tell her the story of how I met my first spiritual mentor when I was 18 years old. His name is Avanti Kumar, and I've written about our adventures in several of my books. Avanti was a fellow student at Birmingham City University. He was an urban mystic. He seemed to have a normal life, and yet he wasn't like anyone I had met before. Avanti introduced me to metaphysics and meditation.

"You are the Buddha, and everyone is waiting for you to remember this," Avanti told me, during one of our many conversations at our favorite coffee shop. He qualified his statement by explaining that we are all Buddha. The name Buddha is a Sanskrit term for *awakened one*—someone who remembers his or her unconditioned nature. Avanti taught me that there is a still, small voice inside each of us that is our real voice and that the more willing we are to listen to this voice, the easier it is to hear it.

Like Louise, I have learned to trust this inner voice. I call this voice my Yes. It's a Yes with a capital Y. I'm pretty sure it's the same as Louise's inner ding. I call it my Yes because it is deeply affirming and I feel it has my best interests at heart. It is also constantly supportive and always on hand when I need it. My inner voice feels like a Yes when I experience its presence in my body, my heart, and my thinking. The Yes is what I listen for when I have a decision to make. The Yes helps me recognize and follow the big plan. The Yes is my light on the path.

"My inner ding is life's way of loving me," Louise tells me. I feel the same way about my Yes. Louise consults with her inner ding throughout the day. "In the beginning I used to meditate in order to be able to hear my inner ding," she says. "I found meditation very difficult to begin with. I experienced violent headaches. It was most uncomfortable. I stuck with it, though, and eventually I learned to enjoy meditation. Meditation helped me to listen from within. I found it a big help early on."

When I ask Louise if she still meditates, she tells me about a great exercise she does. "I don't meditate daily now. Just occasionally. When I wake up I go to the mirror and say, 'Tell me what I need to know today.' And then I listen. It's by doing this exercise that I learned to trust that everything I need to know will be revealed to me in the perfect space-time sequence." Louise tells me she often asks the question *What would you have me know?* when she wants guidance on something specific, such as a health issue, a business decision, or a meeting with someone.

Louise's brilliant exercise reminds me of a prayer in *A Course in Miracles* that I call the Guidance Prayer. I have recited it almost every day for the last 20 years. The idea is to be still, make a conscious connection with your inner voice (whatever you call it), and then simply ask:

> What would You have me do?
>
> Where would You have me go?
>
> What would You have me say and to whom?

Love Who You Are

"I am a *Yes* person living in a *Yes* universe," says Louise.

"That sounds wonderful," I tell her. "What do you mean?"

"Life loves us, and this love sustains us and guides us on our adventures. And so the universe is always saying *Yes* to us."

"Love is the inner ding!" I exclaim.

"Yes," says Louise, smiling. "And I am a *Yes* person because I always follow my inner ding."

"Why do we resist following our inner ding?" I ask.

"Children don't hear the word *yes* enough," Louise says. "They hear *no* and *don't* and *stop that* and *do as I say*. The people who say these things heard the same when they were children."

The first word most children learn to speak is *no,* according to research. I was asked to comment on this research for a BBC news show, and I was surprised by the findings. I thought the most common first word would be *Mum* or *Dad.* Perhaps not. Other research says children hear the word *no* up to 400 times a day. Everyone agrees a child needs to hear the word *no,* but not that much. So maybe *no is* the most common first word. In the beginning was the word, and the word was *no*. Our life starts with a no. That's not much of a start, is it? Imagine if the first word we learned to speak was *yes*.

"Every child has an inner ding," says Louise, "but they need to grow up in a loving, positive environment in order to trust this inner voice." Louise goes on to draw a parallel between healthy children in a family and healthy cells in the body. She refers to Bruce Lipton, the developmental biologist who wrote *The Biology of Belief.* Lipton has collated a large body of research showing that the health of a cell depends on the environment it exists in. A loving, positive environment creates health; but a fearful, negative environment causes unrest. "Without a loving, positive environment, a child forgets about the inner ding," says Louise.

Listening to our inner ding is how we learn to love ourselves. It's how we get the courage to live our truth. When we stop listening to our inner ding, it causes us to reject ourselves. Instead of being true to ourselves— being original, if you like—we try to fit in, to please others, to be normal. But we didn't come here to be normal! Being normal is not following your joy. At the end of your life, your guardian angel or Saint Peter or whoever isn't going to ask you, "Were you normal?" They won't make you take a Normal Test!

"We are constantly invited to be who we are," wrote Henry David Thoreau. To do this we must honor our inner wisdom. I have an exercise about inner wisdom that I teach in my eight-week happiness program, *Be Happy*, which is the signature event of my work with The Happiness Project. The exercise is an invitation for everyone in the group to stand up, one by one, and say out loud the following affirmation: *I am a wise person.*

Affirming *I am a wise person* may sound simple to you, but not everyone finds it easy. Many students experience palpitations just hearing about the exercise. They get weak in the knees as they stand up to say, "I am a wise person." They feel strong emotions, and sometimes tears flow. In the review of this exercise, I encourage my students to notice which "self" finds this exercise difficult. Is it the soul bird, the Unconditioned Self; or their self-image?

During one *Be Happy* program, a man called Alan refused to do this exercise. A senior teacher at a large school in London, he is very capable. Yet when it came to his turn to stand up, he couldn't speak, and he put out his hand to me as if to say, "No, I can't." Alan had been very sociable and had participated fully in the program up until that point. I could see that his outstretched hand was a firm *No*. He wasn't ready. And so we moved on. A few days later, I received an e-mail from Alan. Here's an excerpt from what he wrote:

Dear Robert,

Thank you for the Be Happy program, which I have been enjoying immensely. As you know, last weekend was difficult for me . . . I was taken by surprise at my response to the [I Am a Wise Person] exercise. Something in me froze. It said, "No." I couldn't speak . . . I am a teacher whose greatest joy is to help young boys and girls find their voice. The irony is not lost on me. This is my invitation to heal and to love myself. I am a 46-year-old man, and it is never too late to be a wise person! I want you to know that I am willing to honor the wisdom that you say is in each of us. "I am a wise person." "I am a wise person." "I am a wise person." I am standing up as I type these words! . . . Tears are rolling down my cheeks . . . "I am a wise person." I know this is only in writing . . . I ask that the next time we meet you will give me a chance to say out

loud—to the whole group—"I am a wise person."
It's important for me to do this . . .

Blessings,

Alan

The habit of self-rejection takes control when you play deaf to the wise voice of your true self. You stop listening from within. You override what your body is telling you. You ignore the internal memos from your heart. You don't listen to the song of the soul bird. You move away from yourself. Do you recognize the face in the mirror? Is it really you? Subtly or not so subtly, we give up on ourselves. We tell ourselves we don't matter. We stop believing in ourselves, and we stop caring. "Not being conscious of oneself as spirit is despair," said Søren Kierkegaard.

When you stop following your inner voice, you become estranged from yourself. You forget who you are, and you have no way of knowing what you really want. Like everyone else, you pursue happiness, you chase success, and you look for love, but your loss of inner guidance means you end up looking in the wrong places. You are full of desire, but can you tell the difference between a genuine holy longing and a conditioned response to marketing and advertising? You won't ever get enough of what you didn't really want in the first place. Do you know what you really want to say yes to?

"Every time I hear the word *should*, a bell goes off in my head," says Louise. When you hear yourself say, "I should do . . ." or "I should be . . ." or "I should have . . ." you need to ask yourself, "Who is saying this?" Is this the voice of your Unconditioned Self? Are you really following your joy? Or is this the voice of your ego? "The more you drop *should* from your list, the less noise you experience in your head, and the easier it gets to hear your inner ding again," says Louise.

When we reject ourselves, we are terrified of being rejected by others. If they, too, reject us, there is no one left to love us. We do our best to make ourselves into someone acceptable and loveable. We twist ourselves into shapes that will hopefully please others. We take on roles like helper and martyr and star, in an effort to win love and success. But there's always a nagging feeling that something is missing. Until you accept yourself—and say yes to who you really are—you will always feel like something is missing from your life.

Saying yes is really about meeting the deepest part of you. It's about saying yes to your secret beauty, to your soul nature, and to your creativity. This is what you have to be faithful to. This is what loving yourself is all about. This is the real work of your life. The Persian poet Rumi gave the world a poem called "Say Yes Quickly." He wrote,

> Inside you
> there's an artist you
> don't know about . . .
> Is what I say true? Say yes quickly,
> if you know, if you've known it
> from before the beginning of the universe.

The Sacred Yes

One week before Louise and I were due to start writing *Life Loves You,* I received an e-mail from the author Sandy Newbigging asking me to write a fore-word for his book *Mind Calm.* I felt honored to be asked, but I thought I didn't have the time and needed to keep my focus on this book. I e-mailed Sandy to say my answer would have to be no, but somehow I ended up saying yes. It wasn't an I-should yes, or an I-must yes, or even a be-kind yes. It was a truthful yes. Or what I call my Big Yes—with a capital Y.

Another name for this Yes is my Sacred Yes. I sense this Yes in my belly (gut instinct), I feel it in my heart, and I hear it in my head. When it shows up, I feel like I have almost no choice whether to follow it. This is the "Yes" that simply feels true. To go against it would be inauthentic. I'm so glad I agreed to read Sandy's book. It is full of rich insights. And there's one line in particular that has been so helpful for writing *Life Loves You*. It speaks to me every day. It's the sort of thing my inner voice would say to me:

Let the loving hand of the universe guide you.

"All I've ever done is listen to my inner ding and said yes," Louise tells me as she reflects on her career as a writer and teacher. "I never meant to write a book. My first book, the little blue book *Heal Your Body*, was just a list I compiled. Someone suggested I make it into a book. And I said yes. I had no idea how to publish a book, but helping hands appeared along the way. It was just a little adventure." Little did she realize that her "little adventure" would be a bestseller and the catalyst for a self-help revolution in publishing.

Louise's story about giving talks follows a similar pattern. "Someone invited me to give a talk and I said yes. I had no idea what I'd say, but as soon as I said yes I felt guided along the way." First came talks, then workshops, and then the Hayrides. "A few gay men regularly attended my workshops," Louise recalls. "Then one day I was asked if I'd be willing to start a group for people with AIDS. I said, 'Yes, let's get together and see what happens.'" Louise had no idea where the Hayrides would take her. There wasn't a grand marketing plan. She didn't target appearing on *The Oprah Winfrey Show* and *The Phil Donahue Show*. "I followed my heart," says Louise.

Saying Yes is a willingness to show up. "The big question is whether you are going to be able to say a hearty yes to your adventure," said Joseph Campbell, author of *The Hero's Journey*. The Sacred Yes is about the big plan for your life. It's not about ambition; it's about purpose. It's not about profit; it's about passion. It's not about self-gain; it's about service. The Sacred Yes is about being willing to take to the open road, as Walt Whitman described it.

Saying Yes is an act of faith. Sometimes we don't know why we say yes. We don't have the full picture; and sometimes we can't even see the next step. It's only after we say yes that the next step appears. And it's only after we say yes that we realize there is help along the way. In the PBS special *Joseph Campbell and the Power of Myth*, Bill Moyers interviews Campbell about the need for faith when we follow our purpose. At one point, Moyers asks Campbell if he's ever had the experience of being "helped by hidden hands" on his own journey. Campbell replies,

> All the time. It is miraculous . . . If you do follow your bliss you put yourself on a kind of track that has been there all the while, waiting for you, and the life that you ought to be living is the one you are living. When you can see that, you begin to meet people who are in your field of bliss, and they open doors to you. I say, follow your bliss and don't be afraid, and doors will open where you didn't know they were going to be.

Saying Yes is having an open mind. The Sacred Yes is about dropping your fear, your unworthiness, your cynicism, your psychology, and allowing your soul to speak to you. The Sacred Yes is a surrender. "Ever since I put my foot on the spiritual pathway, it's as though I've had nothing to do with my life. Life has taken over and it's led me all the way. I don't lead. I follow the lead," Louise tells me.

Saying Yes is a journey, not a goal. You say yes not because you are trying to get somewhere but because it's what's in front of you. In *You Can Create an Exceptional Life*, Louise tells Cheryl Richardson, "So often people ask about how I started Hay House. They want to know every detail from the day I began up to today. My answer is always the same: I answered the phone and opened the mail. I did what was before me." The journey is the goal.

Saying Yes is being present in your life. When I was 18 years old, I received two letters in the mail on the same day. One was an invitation to study in a three-year program at Birmingham City University; the other was an acceptance letter for a one-year post-graduate course in journalism at the University of Portsmouth. I was young and ambitious. I wanted to take the fast-track course in journalism, but everything in my body, my heart, and my head said yes to the slow boat to Birmingham. This is where I met Avanti Kumar, my first mentor. This is where I began my spiritual path.

I've often wondered how my life would have unfolded if I hadn't followed my Yes to Birmingham. I asked Louise about this once. She said, "Your Yes will always find you, wherever you are." I love her answer. To me, Louise is saying that following your Yes isn't about getting somewhere, and it isn't about making the right decisions. It's about being present. It's about being authentic. It's about being willing to be led. And it's about looking in the mirror and liking what you see. That's the journey.

PRACTICE 3:
My Affirmation Board

"The oldest, shortest words—*yes* and *no*—are those that require the most thought," the Greek mathematician Pythagoras ostensibly said. Yes and no are woven into the fabric of our daily life. They are the basic mathematics of our psychology. Our thinking is made up of yes and no. These two words are our essential binary code. We speak these words every day. They shape our experience all day long. They are behind every choice we make. They are in every decision we make. Everything is a yes or a no—or a maybe—a little bit of both.

I remember the first time I consciously thought about my relationship to yes and no. I was 26 years old, and I was working for the local health authority in Birmingham, England. I was running a clinic called Stress Busters. The director for public health asked if I would teach a course on assertiveness. The psychologist who had previously taught it was retiring. "Yes," I said. Not because I knew much about assertiveness. I didn't. But the subject interested me, and I wanted to learn more.

Early on in my research on assertiveness, I noticed that the main focus was on saying no. I read articles with titles like "How to Say No" and "Saying No with Confidence" and "The Art of Saying No." I also came across slogans like *Just Say No* and *No means No*. Curiously, there was little mention of the word *yes*. After a few weeks of research, I presented my course, which I called *Assertive, I AM*. The first lesson was called "The Power of Yes." I started with yes because I was developing a theory, which was:

The better you are at saying yes, the
better you will be at saying no.

"Most people start with what they don't want,"
says Louise. "They say, 'I don't want the relationship I am in,' or 'I don't want the job I've got,' or 'I
don't want to live where I am living.'" This is a start
at least, but it's not as powerful as putting your attention and energy on what you want to say yes to.
Louise warns, "The more we dwell on what we don't
want, the more we get it." This is a terrible irony, but
it's true. Saying no may signal a fresh start the first
time you say it, but you don't go anywhere until you
start to say yes.

Some people sort by the negatives, so to speak.
No is the position they take in life. Their first answer
to everything is no or at least maybe, but seldom yes.
This might be because of their personality type or a
reaction to their history. I once had a coaching client
called Susan. Our second session was an inquiry into
the question *What do I want?* Susan said, "I can think
of lots of things I want to say no to, but that's not
the same as knowing what I want to say yes to, is it?"
"No," I replied. Susan had to be patient with herself.
Eventually, the yesses began to flow.

Some people say yes to too many things. Until you know what you really want to say yes to, you will continue to say yes to everything else. This will cause you to experience inner doubt, to be torn between contradictory goals, to get distracted and scattered, to feel compromised, to be exhausted, to get into unhealthy sacrifice, and to give your power away. As you get clearer about the Sacred Yesses of your life, you experience a sense of empowerment and grace that helps you to live a truly blessed life.

This brings us to the third spiritual practice for *Life Loves You*—a practice we call *My Affirmation Board*.

An affirmation board is a self-portrait. It's a presentation of everything you say yes to. The form of your affirmation board is entirely up to you, of course. You might do a collage of hand-drawn images, or pictures cut out of magazines or printed off the Internet. You might prefer to do a written list. Maybe you'd like to do a mind map. Whatever you do, keep it to one page.

You create your affirmation board by listening within. You are listening for your Sacred Yesses. These Sacred Yesses belong to you. They're not your parents' yesses or your partner's, your children's, or anybody else's. They're not about what you *should* do with your life; they are about following your joy. They affirm what you love, what you believe in, and what you cherish and value. They are about you living your truth.

Louise and I have noticed that people's first attempts at creating an affirmation board often focus on having and getting. We encourage you to make sure your Sacred Yesses are more than just a shopping list. You might include developing a quality like courage, gratitude, or forgiveness, for instance. Maybe you want to practice a skill like meditation, yoga, painting, or cooking. Ask yourself, "What do I want to learn?" and "What do I want to experience?" Include your favorite affirmation or a personal mantra, for instance. The key is to express yourself, heart and soul. To focus on *being* rather than *doing*.

Louise and I encourage you to give your *My Affirmation Board* plenty of time. Express yourself. Be creative. Feel free to experiment. It's not about getting it right. And it's not about creating something that looks good.

If you want, you can share your board with a coach or a trusted friend. It's good to get feedback. Maybe they will point out something obvious that you've missed. Finally, make sure that your affirmation board is about what you say yes to *today,* not someday in the future. Remember, this isn't about chasing happiness; it is about following your joy.

CHAPTER 4

Forgiving the Past

Fear binds the world. Forgiveness sets it free.

A Course in Miracles

The wind from the east has arrived. A storm is blowing across California. San Diego has been a desert for months. Now, clouds hang low over the city. The squalls keep coming. The trees in Balboa Park are shaking at their roots. The stale hot air has gone. The healing power of rain is most welcome. "I hope it rains all weekend," Louise tells me. "The rain is making everything new."

It's Friday evening, and I've just flown in from London. The descent to the San Diego airport was full of bumps and sudden drops. The landing was rough. Our plane bounced along the runway before it came to a stop. It feels good to be on the ground. Louise and I are sitting in front of a warm fire in her home, catching up on each other's news. We're happy to be together, and yet this time it feels different. We're both aware that we are at the midpoint of our journey with *Life Loves You*. All along we've known that this chapter represents the heart of the book. The theme is forgiveness.

Writing a book is never just about writing a book. I wouldn't write as often as I do if that were all it was. Writing is like looking into a mirror. This is especially true when you focus on big subjects like happiness, healing, and love. Writing helps you to pay attention. It helps you to see what is in front of you. When you stay with it, you experience a heightened sense of awareness—just as in meditation. This new awareness is often disturbing and liberating. It blows through you, rearranging your molecules. Writing, at its best, sets you free.

I've been writing for several weeks now. The words *Life loves you* are my mirror. They are my inquiry, and I'm taking them deep into my body, my heart, and my thoughts. These three words—*Life loves you*—are now firmly fixed in my awareness. They are often there to greet me upon waking. They pop into my mind throughout the day. They are always nearby, no matter what I'm doing. In bed at night, I can feel these words circling over me, ready to take me off to sleep.

I've also been tracking my responses to *Life loves you*. Each time I hear these three words, I can hear my soul saying, "Yes." Sometimes it's a gentle whisper, and other times it's a joyous shout. With each Yes I feel physically strong and deeply heartened. I know life is spurring me on. That said, I'm also aware of other voices that call out from the dark corners of my mind. These voices are more cynical. They are full of hurt. *Life loves you* sounds like mere words to them, and the words are too good to be true.

"The first time you said *Life loves you* to me was probably not the first time," I tell Louise.

"Probably not," says Louise with a wry smile.

"It's taken me a while to let myself hear these words," I admit.

"Not everyone can hear them," she says.

"Sometimes they sound like the gospel truth," I say, "but other times, they feel like only a positive affirmation."

"I know how that feels," says Louise.

"Why do we find it difficult to hear these words?" I ask her.

"We don't believe them," says Louise.

"Why is that?"

"We don't believe in ourselves."

"Why not?"

"Guilt!"

Guilt is a loss of innocence. It's what we experience when we forget the basic truth *I am loveable*. It comes with the basic fear *I am not loveable*. It's a belief in unworthiness. When we lose sight of our innocence—which is our true nature—we believe we don't deserve love. We long for love, but we turn away from it when it comes, because we feel unworthy. Our feeling of unworthiness is what causes us not only to feel unloveable but also to behave in unloving ways toward ourselves and others.

Guilt is a fear that *once upon a time I was loveable, but I'm not anymore.* Guilt always comes with a story. The story might be about what you did to someone or what someone did to you. It's a story based on what happened in the past. The story has normally finished by now, and yet it can feel like a never-ending tale.

We can become so identified with our guilty story, we're afraid to let it go. *Who would I be without this story and this unworthiness?* we wonder. The answer is, you would be innocent again. You would feel wholly loveable.

The guilt story is something everyone can relate to. We each have our own special version of it. The story begins inside us, and then we project it onto the world. It's a story told in all the major mythologies of the world. The basic fear *I am not loveable* is our mythology. We use it to judge ourselves, criticize ourselves, and reject ourselves. From this mythology comes superstition, which is the fear that God is judging you, the world isn't safe, and life does not love you.

The guilt story is always based on a case of mistaken identity. The protagonist of the guilt story has forgotten who she is. She has lost sight of her innocence. Like Adam in the Garden of Eden and Sleeping Beauty, you fall asleep. Like Oedipus and the Frog Prince, you dream you are a victim of a curse. Like the Fisherman's Daughter and Theseus, you forget about your heritage. Like the Ugly Duckling and the Beast (in *Beauty and the Beast*), you cannot see your true beauty. Like Odysseus and the Prodigal Son, you have to make a journey home.

Innocence exists forever in the Unconditioned Self. The ego—your mistaken identity—doesn't believe this. It feels unworthy and believes in guilt. The ego believes that if you're guilty enough you can buy back your innocence. Unfortunately, there's no exchange rate between guilt and love. *No amount of guilt can buy any amount of love.* The guilt story ends only when the protagonist gives up unworthiness. Often it takes an angel, or a prince or princess, to show you your innocence again. When you claim your innocence, it creates healing for everyone, which is a miracle to the ego.

"Helping people to heal guilt is the most important work I do," says Louise. "As long as you believe you are unworthy and keep making yourself guilty, you stay stuck in a story that does no one any good at all." When I ask Louise if guilt has any positive purpose, she tells me, "The only positive function of guilt is that it tells you you've forgotten who you really are and that it's time to remember." Guilt is a warning sign, an alarm that sounds when you are not in alignment with your true nature and acting with love.

"Guilt doesn't heal anything," says Louise.

"Explain that, please," I ask.

"Feeling guilty about what you did, or what someone

did to you, doesn't make the past go away. Guilt doesn't make the past better."

"Are you saying we should never feel guilt?"

"No," says Louise. "I'm saying that when you feel guilt or believe that you are unworthy, you should use it as a sign that you need to heal."

"How do we heal guilt, Louise?"

"Forgiveness."

Loving Your Inner Child

Louise and I are sitting together in front of a mirror that hangs on a wall in her living room. It's a big mirror, about five feet long and three feet high. We are both in full view. There is nowhere to hide. It's 9:30 A.M., and we have a full day of conversation and exploration in front of us. Louise sips her homemade green smoothie, which is full of goodness. I'm drinking my coffee, which, I maintain, is also full of goodness. Coffee is a delivery device for the Holy Spirit, I say. I press the record button on my computer. We are ready to talk about forgiveness.

"Forgiveness is such a big subject, Louise. Where do we start?"

"Loving your inner child," Louise says in that matter-of-fact way of hers.

"Why do we start there?"

"Until you love your inner child you will have no idea how loveable you are, and you won't see how much life loves you," she explains.

"That's profound," I say, taking a sip of coffee.

"That's because it's true," she says with a smile.

Louise Hay is a pioneer of inner-child therapy. She's taught inner-child work with individuals and groups for 40 years. She's written about loving the inner child in all her major books. She's published meditations on healing the inner child. By contrast, I am a beginner. I've experienced some inner-child therapy personally, but that was a long time ago. I knew we would meet this subject eventually, so I enrolled myself in a course of inner-child counseling. I did this for myself, as part of my own journey with this book. I'd had my fourth session just before I flew out to be with Louise.

"Loving the inner child is what helps us find our innocence again," says Louise.

"How do we love the inner child?" I ask.

"The same way you love your adult self," she says.

"By ceasing all self-judgment," I say.

"Babies are not bad people. No one is born guilty. No one is unworthy," says Louise firmly, like a fierce, protective lioness.

"Do you really mean *everyone*?"

"Every baby is created out of goodness," Louise says. "It's only when we forget about our goodness that we start to feel guilty and unworthy."

The loss of innocence causes us to lose sight of our basic goodness. This basic goodness is recognized in many spiritual and philosophical traditions. Matthew Fox, founder of Creation Spirituality, calls this basic goodness our *original blessing*. He draws on a lineage of basic goodness expounded by Christian mystics like Julian of Norwich, who wrote,

> As the body is clothed in cloth
> and the muscles in the skin
> and the bones in the muscles
> and the heart in the chest,
>
> so are we, body and soul,
> clothed in the Goodness of God
> and enclosed.

The basic truth *I am loveable* is keeper of the flame. When we remember the basic truth about ourselves, we feel innocent, we feel worthy, and we extend this goodness to each other. When we doubt that we are loveable, we meet the basic fear *I am not loveable*. This fear causes us to feel bad about ourselves. It conjures up the myth of inadequacy: *I am not good enough*. The voices in the dark corners of our mind declare *I am bad* and *There's something wrong with me*. We feel like damaged goods, and we project this guilt onto our dealings with others. The shame of our ego obscures the innocence of our soul.

"Since I've become a parent, I notice how much pressure children are put under to be good," I tell Louise.

"I notice that, too," she says.

"Most modern parenting manuals focus on instilling good behavior in children. We don't trust that children have any innate goodness," I say.

"If the pressure to be a good girl and a good boy is too great, it can cause us to feel unloveable," says Louise.

"All those good-behavior messages can make you want to have a *Bad Tuesday*," I say.

"What's a *Bad Tuesday*?" Louise asks.

"It's a chapter in *Mary Poppins*. The little boy,

Michael, is so fed up with having to be good that he behaves badly all day," I explain.

"We all know what that's like," says Louise with a smile.

"Too many *should*s and *must*s block the flow of innate goodness," I say.

"When a parent has lost touch with their own goodness, it's impossible for them to trust the goodness that lives in their children," says Louise.

One Saturday morning not so long ago, my children and I set out on an adventure. We had the whole day to ourselves, as Hollie was attending a program on Biographical Counseling, which maps the phases of your life, including early childhood. Bo, Christopher, and I went in search of the golden pheasant that lives in the Royal Botanic Gardens, also known as Kew Gardens. Most members of the Kew Friends have never seen the golden pheasant, but we have. We've seen it many times.

On our way we stopped off at our favorite health food shop in Kew called Oliver's Wholefoods. Bo and I picked delicious snacks from the shelves and dropped them into a basket that Christopher was wheeling around. The basket was as big as he was, and it soon became quite heavy with lots of healthy treats. Christopher manfully pulled the basket toward the counter. He insisted on doing this by himself, and he had to heave it with all his might.

While we were standing in line, ready to pay for our goodies, a friendly-looking lady we did not know engaged us in conversation. "What's your name?" she asked, looking at Bo. Bo told her. "Are you a good little girl?" she asked. Bo didn't answer. The friendly-looking lady turned to Christopher. "What's your name?" she asked. "Bisterfer," he said, which is nearly Christopher, especially when you are only a toddler. "Oh," she said. "And are you a good little boy?"

The friendly-looking lady looked into the basket that Christopher was holding. "My goodness!" she exclaimed. "You must have been a good girl and a good boy for Daddy to get you all these treats." She smiled at me as she said this. Bo wasn't smiling. I knew what she was thinking. I wasn't sure what Christopher was making of all this. I hoped it was flying over his head. "Well, I'm sure you are very good children. Only very good children get treats," she said.

We packed our treats into my rucksack and walked out of the shop. After just a few paces, Bo gave a firm tug on my coat.

"Daddy, we need to talk," she told me.

"I thought we might," I said.

"You see, I don't want to be a good girl," she said most adamantly.

"What would you like to be?"

"I'd like to be a lovely girl."

"What's a lovely girl like?"

"It's like this," she told me. "When I go out people say to me 'You're a lovely girl,' and all I have to say is 'Thank you.'"

"Bo, you are a lovely girl," I said.

"Thank you," she said with a big smile.

One of the themes I've been exploring in my inner-child counseling is the pressure I put on myself when I was young to be "a good little boy." Early on, I worked out that good little boys didn't get shouted at, didn't get hit, and didn't get into trouble. I hoped that if I was always good and never bad, my parents would never say to me, "We are so disappointed in you." I hated it when they said that. However, being good full-time is hard work. You have to suppress a lot of feelings. You can't always speak the truth. Sometimes you have to lie. And that feels bad.

Trying to be a good little boy is difficult for lots of reasons. For starters, adults have different versions of what *good* is. Your mum and your dad might not agree on what good is. Your grandparents probably don't agree with what your parents think. Your teachers have their own ideas, and so too do your friends. And everyone changes his or her mind all the time anyway, and that just makes you mad. You can't win. It's so unfair. But you tell yourself that you mustn't say anything because that's not good.

The more you try to be a good little boy or a good little girl, the more you have to put on an act. Putting on an act is not innocent. It's a calculated attempt to win love and approval, or, simply to stay out of trouble. Being good is just one act. Other acts include being strong ("brave little soldier"), being helpful ("my little helper"), being nice ("my little angel"), and being a little adult ("a big girl"). More acts include being an invisible child, the family hero, a scapegoat, a problem child, and the entertainer.

"I tried to be a good little girl at first," Louise tells me. "But that got me unwanted attention from my stepfather. In the end, I tried to be an invisible child in order to make myself safe." Whatever act we choose, it causes us to feel estranged from our basic goodness.

The basic fear *I am not loveable* morphs into a belief that *I must deserve love*. When we identify with this erroneous belief, love ceases to feel natural and uncon-ditional. Instead, we fear that love is a prize that must be earned, deserved, and achieved somehow, but only if we are worthy.

We take our childhood acts into adulthood with us. These acts turn into roles we play out in relation-ships. Without our basic goodness, we are lost. We search outside of ourselves for love. We look for a prince or princess who can save us from our basic fear of being unloveable. We are trapped in a dungeon of unworthiness, hoping someone will rescue us.

In the movie *Shrek the Third*, Sleeping Beauty, Snow White, Rapunzel, Cinderella, Doris the Ugly Stepsister, and Princess Fiona and her mother, Queen Lillian, are imprisoned in a tower by Prince Charming. Fiona wants the ladies to plot their own escape. "Ladies, as-sume the position!" says Snow White. Instantly, Sleep-ing Beauty falls asleep, Snow White lies down in a coffin pose, and Cinderella gazes dreamily into space. "What are you doing?" shouts Princess Fiona. Sleeping Beauty snaps awake and says, "Waiting to be rescued," and then falls back asleep again. "You have got to be kidding me!" says Princess Fiona.

In *Pretty Woman*, a modern-day fairy tale, Julia Roberts plays Vivian Ward, a Hollywood prostitute hired by a wealthy businessman, Edward Lewis, played by Richard Gere, to be his escort for some social engagements. Business soon turns to love. Lewis thinks he is rescuing Ward, but Ward has other ideas. In the final scene, Prince Edward arrives in a white limo calling out to Princess Vivian. He climbs the fire escape to her top-floor apartment. When he finally reaches her, he asks, "So what happened after he climbed up the tower and rescued her?" Vivian replies, "She rescues him right back."

The victim and the rescuer are both playing a role in an effort to win love. The point is, there can be no happily-ever-after in any of these stories—or in any of our relationships—until we claim our basic goodness for ourselves. Everyone can help us with our quest. Indeed, we will need help along the way. Ultimately, however, it must be our decision to reclaim our basic goodness. This decision is a journey in itself. It is a journey of forgiveness, a journey that takes us back to love again.

"Loving the inner child is about forgiving ourselves for our loss of innocence and loss of goodness," says Louise. "The truth is, we all did the best we could with what we knew at every stage of our childhood. And yet, we may still be judging ourselves and punishing ourselves for not having done it better, for making mistakes, for abandoning ourselves, for upsetting others, and for not being a good enough boy or girl. Until we forgive ourselves, we will be trapped in a prison of righteous resentment. Forgiveness is the only way out of this prison. Forgiveness sets us free."

Louise and I close our conversation about forgiveness and loving the inner child with a meditation in front of the mirror. This meditation happened spontaneously, but I've reconstructed it here. You might like to follow it for your own inner-child meditation. "Encourage everyone to do this meditation in front of the mirror," Louise tells me. I assure her I will put it in writing!

We recommend that you do this meditation sitting in front of a mirror. Place your hands over your heart. Take a deep breath. See yourself through the eyes of love. And speak to yourself with love.

I am loveable and life loves me.
I forgive myself for all the times I've been
afraid I am not loveable.
I am loveable and life loves me.

I forgive myself for judging myself and
for not believing in my goodness.
I am loveable and life loves me.

I forgive myself for feeling unworthy and
for believing I don't deserve love.
I am loveable and life loves me.
I forgive myself for all the times I've
criticized and attacked myself.
I am loveable and life loves me.

I forgive myself for rejecting and
giving up on myself.
I am loveable and life loves me.
I forgive myself for doubting myself and
for not trusting in me.
I am loveable and life loves me.

I forgive myself for my mistakes.
I am loveable and life loves me.
I ask for forgiveness so that I can learn.
I accept forgiveness so that I can grow.
I am loveable and life loves me.

Forgiving Your Parents

"Who's been the hardest person for you to forgive?" I ask Louise.

"That would have to be my mother and my stepfather, but mostly my stepfather," she replies.

"What's been the greatest gift of forgiving them?"

"Forgiveness set me free," she says.

"What do you mean?"

"Well, I ran away from a home full of physical violence and sexual abuse. I had to run away in order to survive. But I soon ran into more trouble, including more abuse," says Louise.

"Running away only gets you so far."

"Yes. And no matter how much distance I put between me and my childhood, and me and my stepfather, I couldn't escape," she says.

"Escape from what?"

"I carried enormous guilt. I did what all children do: I blamed myself for what happened. I took this guilt into my adult relationships. I bumbled along. I was a dutiful wife. I lived my life as best I could, but I wasn't fully alive," she says.

"You were functioning but not flourishing."

"Exactly. And after my husband asked for a divorce,

I couldn't even function. Then I was diagnosed with vaginal cancer. This was when I decided to stop running," says Louise.

"Were you tired of running by then?"

"Yes. And I knew that the cancer was caused by my guilt and by my anger and resentment at being physically, mentally, and sexually abused as a child," she says.

"How did you know that?"

"My inner ding," she says, pointing to her heart. "For the first time in my life I really paid attention to my inner voice, and it led me to the Church of Religious Science and to metaphysics and to forgiveness."

"And forgiveness set you free."

"I felt like I'd been wearing one of those prison release tags that prisoners get when they're released on parole for good behavior, and forgiveness was the key that meant I could take the tag off and be free," she says.

"What was your first step to freedom?"

"Well, first I had to stop running. Then I had to look in the mirror and confront my past. What happened with my stepfather was not okay, but it was also not okay that I was still punishing myself for it," says Louise.

"Eventually, we have to choose between holding on to resentments and being free."

"Yes. And at first I didn't want to forgive, but I also didn't want to have cancer, and I wanted to be free from my past," says Louise.

"So, how did you get out of jail?"

"I read in *A Course in Miracles* that all disease comes from a state of nonforgiveness and that forgiveness can heal every guilt and every fear. I asked my inner ding if this was true, and it said, '*Yes!*'" she shouts joyously.

"And the truth will set you free!"

"The willingness to forgive opened the prison door. Stepping out of the prison took courage, and I got a lot of support from some excellent teachers and therapists. They showed me that forgiveness is an act of self-love. I was doing this for me," she says.

"*A Course in Miracles* states, 'All forgiveness is a gift to yourself.'"

"I had to forgive in order to set myself free. So I forgave myself for allowing guilt and resentment to harm my body. I forgave myself for feeling unloveable. I forgave myself for the guilt I carried. I forgave my parents. I forgave my past. And in return, I was given this life, the one I've been living for 40 years now.

Forgiveness gave me a chance to be Louise Hay and to be the real me. That is the real gift of forgiveness."

"Amen."

Your relationship with your parents was your first mirror in this lifetime. Your parents' capacity to mirror love to you was influenced by how loveable they felt and by how much they let life love them. What you saw in your parents' mirroring was what you believed to be true. Since this was your first mirror, it influences what you see in every other mirror, and in all your other relationships. In the healing journey, you return to the first mirror. Here you have to be willing to look again with new eyes that are not clouded by judgment, guilt, and resentment. With new eyes what you see in the mirror changes, and these changes are reflected in every other mirror, too.

You must not underestimate the influence your parents have had on your life. Your body was created from their bodies. They gave you your name, the one you believe is yours. Their language is your mother tongue, most likely. Their nationality is your nationality, most commonly. Their religion is yours by birth, most probably. Your politics might also be theirs. Your prejudices might also be theirs. Your fears might also be theirs. As huge as this parental influence is, you also must not underestimate the holy power within you that spurs you on to live your own life.

A beautiful teaching on parenting comes from Kahlil Gibran, the Lebanese poet: In his book *The Prophet*, he encourages us to "know the secrets of your heart" and to "love one another, but not make a bond of love." He reminded parents:

> Your children are not your children.
> They are the sons and daughters of Life's
>   longing for itself.
> They come through you but not from you,
> And though they are with you yet they
>   belong not to you.

With only a few changes to the words, this sage advice can be extended to children to help them live their own life. My rewrite says:

> Your parents are not your parents.
> They are the sons and daughters of Life's
>   longing for itself.
> You come through them but not from them,
> And though they are with you yet
>   you belong not to them.

Your parents are your first mirrors, and they are also your first teachers. "We learn a lot about how to forgive or not forgive from our parents," says Louise. Typically, children adopt their parents' attitudes as their own at first. Children learn mostly by imitation in the early years. Your parents' teachings are your first "bible," so to speak. Some of their teachings will be helpful to you, but not all of them. No doubt, you will need to unlearn some teachings in order to hear your own holy voice.

While Louise and I have been writing this book, we've also been designing a public program called *Life Loves You*. One of the modules is on family attitudes and forgiveness. In this module, you explore what your mother and father taught you about forgiveness as you were growing up. We designed a questionnaire to help you with your inquiry. Here's a sample of the questions:

Was your mother a forgiving person?
What did your mother teach you about forgiveness?
How did your mother handle conflict?
How did your mother heal her grievances?
How did your mother let you know all was forgiven?
How did your mother ask for forgiveness?

Was your father a forgiving person?

What did your father teach you about forgiveness?

How did your father handle conflict?

How did your father heal his grievances?

How did your father let you know all was forgiven?

How did your father ask for forgiveness?

Our parents give us our first opportunity to practice forgiveness. This is true, no matter how loving your parents were. The class on forgiveness begins at birth for both parent and child. This class is 24/7 with only a few short breaks, mostly for sleep. Parent and child are both student and teacher. The syllabus is full of new learning. There are good days and bad days. And every day there's another opportunity to practice forgiveness.

Where there is love, there is forgiveness. With love, forgiveness is so natural it doesn't even need a name. Love is forgiving. Love dissolves grievances before they turn to poison. Love heals you quicker than a wound appears. Love makes amends so you don't have to take a wrong turn. And yet, we all fall out of love, both with ourselves and with each other. We forget the basic truths that we are loveable and that life loves us. This forgetfulness obscures our vision and distorts our mirror. This is when the need for forgiveness arises.

Every family has a forgiveness story. This story is part of the human drama and our personal drama. Parents never fully live up to their ideal self, and so they must learn self-forgiveness if they are to grow into truly loving men and women. Children have to learn to forgive their parents for being exactly how they were and not some other ideal; otherwise, children won't grow up to be healthy adults who are free to be their true self. Remember: Your relationship with your parents is your first mirror. Therefore:

What you don't forgive your parents for
you do to yourself.

What you don't forgive your parents for
you accuse others of doing to you.

What you don't forgive your parents for
you do to others.

What you don't forgive your parents for
your children will accuse you of
doing to them.

Letting Go of Grievances

Louise and I are well into our second day of conversations on forgiveness. The rain is still falling in San Diego. Strong gusts of wind blow against the windows. The low-flying clouds move fast through the air. Periodically, small patches of blue break through the ceiling of gray. The sun is up there somewhere. We've been indoors most of the time, doing our inner work, save for one trip to Whole Foods, to stock up for dinner. Our conversations have been intense, full of insight, and healing. There's always something new to learn about forgiveness. A little willingness goes a long way.

"Louise, what is real forgiveness?" I ask, digging for more insights.

"Forgiveness is letting go," she says.

"Letting go of what?"

"The past, guilt, resentment, fear, anger, anything that is not love," she says.

"That feels good," I tell her.

"Real forgiveness feels good," says Louise, smiling.

"So, what helps us to let go?"

"Well, in my case, what helped me was understanding my parents' childhoods," she says.

"What did you learn?"

"My stepfather had a very troubled childhood. Both parents physically abused him. He was punished repeatedly for not doing well at school. He had a twin brother who went to an insane asylum. He never mentioned his mother. He fled from Switzerland to the United States at an early age. He ran away, like I had to."

"How did this understanding help you?"

"Understanding doesn't condone what happened," she says emphatically. "Crucially, it gave me perspective. It helped me to have compassion for myself and, later on, for him as well. Most of all, it helped me to let go of the belief that it was all my fault."

"Forgiveness really is letting go," I say as I let this sink in.

"Yes, it is," she agrees.

Healing is a release from the past. Everyone's past includes some disaster and pain. There is only one way to survive your past, and that is to practice forgiveness. Without forgiveness, you can't get past your history. You feel stuck. Your life isn't moving on, because you haven't moved on. The present can't comfort you because you're not really here. The future looks like more of the same because you see only your past. In reality, the past is over, but it isn't over in your mind. That's why you're still in pain.

Until you forgive, you will keep giving your future to the past. However, forgiveness teaches you that, who you truly are has nothing to do with what happened in your past. Your experiences are not your identity. They can have a big effect on you, but they do not define you. What you did to another person or what they did to you is not the end of your story. When you can say, "I am not my past," and "I am willing to forgive my past," you can create a new future. With forgiveness, a new chapter begins.

Healing is a release from guilt. We tell ourselves, "If only I'd done it differently"—or "If they had acted differently"—"I'd be okay now." At one point or another, we've all wished for a different past. Guilt is a somber lesson, but it isn't a solution. When you keep on punishing yourself and attacking others, it changes nothing. Forgiveness can't change what happened in the past, but it can change the meaning you give it. For example, instead of punishing yourself, you can use the past to make amends and be who you really are. Henceforth, the past is no longer a prison; it's an open door.

"Forgiveness taught me that as much as I wanted my past to be different, it was over now," Louise tells me. "Through forgiveness, I was able to use my past to learn, to heal, to grow, and to take responsibility for my life now." What really makes a difference in your life is not what happened in the past but what you do with your past in the present. "The present moment is your point of power," says Louise. "You can create only in this moment now." With forgiveness, you change your relationship to the past, and this changes your relationship to the present and the future.

Healing is a release from fear. *A Course in Miracles* paints a most graphic and disturbing picture of the unforgiving mind. A passage in Lesson 121, "Forgiveness is the key to happiness," states:

> The unforgiving mind is full of fear, and offers love no room to be itself; no place where it can spread its wings in peace and soar above the turmoil of the world. The unforgiving mind is sad, without the hope of respite and release from pain. It suffers and abides in misery, peering about in darkness, seeing not, yet certain of the danger lurking there.

Without forgiveness, there is no end to fear.

"When people say 'I can't forgive,' they usually mean 'I won't forgive,'" says Louise. "And the reason they won't forgive is because they're afraid of forgiveness."

Most fears of forgiveness are what I call theoretical fears. These fears arise before you practice forgiveness, but they disappear once you have forgiven. For example, the fear that forgiveness makes you weak or vulnerable couldn't be further from the truth. Forgiveness sets you free. Similarly, forgiveness doesn't mean you forget what happened in the past; it means you don't forget to live in the present.

Ultimately, the fear of forgiveness is not as frightening as the fear of not forgiving. It's more frightening to hold onto grievances than it is to let them go. It's more frightening to keep punishing yourself than it is to heal and awaken. Carrying grievances is painful. Of course, you have to grieve your past. Without proper grieving, there will be no end to your suffering. At some point, however, not letting go of grievances is really a decision to keep on suffering. Suffering doesn't, by itself, make things better for you or anyone else. Suffering is a wake-up call.

"The present is forgiveness," states *A Course in Miracles*. In the present moment, we let go of the past. In the present moment, we fear nothing. In the present moment, there is no guilt. In the present moment, the meaning of the past can be undone. In the present moment, a new future is born. With forgiveness, we remember the basic truth *I am loveable*. With forgiveness, we let life love us. With forgiveness, we can be a loving presence to the people in our life.

Forgiveness offers us a beautiful vision for the future. With forgiveness, we can spread love from the inside out, to family, friends, strangers, enemies, and the whole world. This is how we end the cycle of fear and pain, judgment and guilt, revenge and attack. This is how we create a better future for our children. William Martin, in his book *The Parent's Tao Te Ching*, gives a wonderful demonstration of how our self-acceptance and our healing helps to heal the future. He writes,

> How do children learn
> to correct their mistakes?
> By watching how you correct yours.
> How do children learn
> to overcome their failures?
> By watching how you overcome yours.
> How do children learn
> to treat themselves with forgiveness?
> By watching you forgive yourself.

Therefore your mistakes,
and your failures
are blessings,
opportunities for the best
in parenting.
And those who point out your mistakes
are not your enemies,
but the most valuable of friends.

PRACTICE 4:
THE FORGIVENESS SCALE

It's Monday morning, and Louise and I are wrapping up our conversation on forgiveness. The storm has passed. San Diego is enjoying clear blue skies and sunshine again. The air feels brand-new, as if it has never been breathed before. It's been a big weekend for us, and we both feel like today is a new beginning.

Forgiveness is a new beginning. It plugs you into the totality of possibilities that exists in love. Its effects can be miraculous. Forgiveness helps you to get clear about your past. It encourages you to be honest about what really happened and to honor the lessons, accept the healing, and receive the blessings. Forgiveness teaches you that staying in pain doesn't make pain go away. Guilt and resentment cannot make amends. Dying doesn't help the living. Forgiveness is the way back to love. Love is what helps you to live again.

"We don't need to know how to forgive. All we need is to be willing to forgive," says Louise. Saying yes to forgiveness is the first step. When you affirm *I say yes to forgiveness,* it activates something in you, and healing begins. Your willingness orchestrates the healing and arranges for you to meet the right people and find the necessary help along the way. As you keep on saying yes to forgiveness, every step of the way, your healing journey takes you from the past into the present and to an entirely new future.

Our spiritual practice for you in this chapter is called *The Forgiveness Scale.* This practice helps you to cultivate the necessary willingness to experience the blessings of total forgiveness. The Forgiveness Scale is based on a scale of 0 to 100 percent. You begin by choosing a person to focus on. You can choose yourself, which is always a good idea. Or you can choose anyone else, even someone with whom you have only a slight grievance. You'll notice there isn't anyone in your life that you don't have a bit of a grievance with.

Prepare yourself as you would for meditation. Ground yourself, breathe fully, and let your body relax. Bring your focus person into your awareness. When you are ready, ask yourself, "From 0 to 100 percent, how much have I forgiven this person?" Record your first answer to this question. Be honest with yourself. The goal here is not to be good, or to get it right, or to be spiritual, or to be nice. You are not trying to play a role. You want to set yourself free. Every answer is a good answer, because it gives you something to work with.

Let's imagine you have chosen yourself as the focus person. And let's say your score is 72 percent. First, notice what it's like to be at 72 percent. How does being at 72 percent affect the way you live your life? How does it affect your happiness, your health, and your success? How does being at 72 percent affect your relationships with others—your capacity to be intimate, to trust, and to forgive? How does being at 72 percent affect your relationship to food, abundance, money, creativity, and your spirituality?

Now here's the next step. In your mind, take the number up from 72 to 80 percent. You can do this one percentage point at a time, if you like. Once you reach 80 percent, affirm *I am willing to forgive myself 80 percent.* Say this a few times and monitor your responses. Notice any physical sensations, any feelings, and any thoughts. Stay here until it feels comfortable. And then keep going further along the scale, to 85 percent and 90 percent and 95 percent.

Every step you take on the Forgiveness Scale helps you to let go of the basic fear *I am not loveable* and to experience the basic truth *I am loveable*. Every step helps you to see that life loves you and that life wants you to be free of guilt, pain, and fear. Every step helps you to experience healing, grace, and inspiration that will benefit you and others.

Imagine being at 100 percent and saying "I am willing to forgive myself 100 percent." The Forgiveness Scale is all about your willingness to release the blocks to forgiveness and to experience love. In a way, you are rehearsing forgiveness. It's an act of imagination. However, imagination is very powerful. "Imagination is everything. It is the preview of life's coming attractions," said Albert Einstein. And so it is.

We recommend that you use the Forgiveness Scale to assess your level of self-forgiveness and forgiveness of others. Ask yourself:

From 0 to 100 percent, how much have I forgiven myself?

From 0 to 100 percent, how much have I forgiven my mother?

From 0 to 100 percent, how much have I forgiven my father?

From 0 to 100 percent, how much have I forgiven my sibling?

From 0 to 100 percent, how much have I forgiven my friend, ex-partner, neighbor?

From 0 to 100 percent, how much have I forgiven everyone?

Always begin with the question "From 0 to 100 percent, how much have I forgiven [myself or name of person]?" Start with the first percentage you thought of and begin your journey along the scale from there. Even a shift of one percent on the Forgiveness Scale will help you let go of the past and create a better future.

We encourage you to do this exercise once a day for seven days. During those seven days, notice what happens in your life. Notice how you show up. Notice how people respond to you. Notice the little miracles. One reason why people often describe forgiveness as a miracle is that when you forgive one person or one thing, it seems to change your relationship to everyone and everything.

Louise and I believe that the Forgiveness Scale is a powerful exercise. Therefore, we strongly recommend that you do not do this exercise alone if you have experienced trauma in your past. Make sure you get the support of a trusted friend, therapist, or coach. Always be gentle with yourself. Forgiveness is an expression of love, and it should be a loving process. Love is the healing power that takes us back to our innocence. Love is the journey home.

CHAPTER 5

Being Grateful Now

*To wake at dawn with a winged
heart and give thanks for
another day of loving.*

KAHLIL GIBRAN, *THE COLLECTED WORKS*

Guess what Louise Hay does first thing when she wakes up each morning? Well, it's not brushing her teeth or going to the toilet. And it's not dancing the rumba. I'm not saying she doesn't do any of those things each morning, but it's not what she does first thing. "On waking, before I open my eyes, I like to thank my bed for a good night's sleep," says

Louise. I ask you, dear reader, who else do you know who does such a thing? Imagine beginning each day with gratitude even before you open your eyes.

"Louise, you're the only person I know who thanks her bed for a good night's sleep," I tell her.

"Well, I'm pleased for you that you've finally met someone who does," she says.

"It's not very normal, is it?" I jest.

"I'm not interested in being normal," she counters.

"Normal is overrated," I say.

"I think so," says Louise.

"So when did you first start to thank your bed for a good night's sleep?"

"Oh, I don't know," she says, as if she's been doing it forever.

"Was it 30 years ago, 40 years ago?" I ask.

"Once upon a time I used to wake up and think, *Oh shit! Another day!*" she says with a big laugh.

"Now that's a powerful affirmation!"

"Yes, and I'd have a shitty day!" she says.

Louise begins her day with gratitude. "It's a great way to start the day," she says. Just as with affirmations, however, she doesn't just do a ten-minute gratitude exercise and then get busy with her day. She makes a point of taking gratitude with her into her day. She has reminders everywhere. Underneath the mirror that hangs on her kitchen wall there's a sign in gold lettering that reads *What are you grateful for today?* Louise practices gratitude with great mindfulness, and she happily expresses her gratitude to everyone and to everything.

"Louise, I've been watching you!" I say.

"Have you?" she replies coyly.

"Yes. And I see that you are in constant dialogue with life," I tell her.

"Am I?" she says.

"Yes. You talk to your bed. You talk to your mirror. You talk to your teacup. You talk to your breakfast bowl. You talk to your computer. You talk to your car. You talk to your clothes. You talk to everything."

"Yes, I do," she says with pride.

"And mostly what you say is 'Thank you.'"

"Well, I'm grateful that my car works well, and that my computer connects me to my friends, and that my clothes feel so nice to wear," she says.

"I think you live an enchanted life," I tell her.

"I am blessed," she says.

Louise hasn't always felt blessed. "There was a time when I wasn't grateful for anything," she tells me. "It didn't occur to me to practice gratitude because I didn't think I had anything to be grateful for." She recalls how her first gratitude exercise was like trying a new affirmation. It didn't feel real to her, and it didn't seem to work. That soon changed, however. "Gratitude opened my eyes to a new way of seeing the world," she explains. "By making gratitude a daily prayer—*Thank you, life; thank you, life*—I learned to trust in life again. I felt loveable again, and I began to see that life really does love me."

Listening to Louise talk about gratitude reminds me of something called basic trust. Basic trust is woven into the fabric of our Unconditioned Self. It's not just a state of mind, it's a way of being. Basic trust allows the soul bird to spread its wings and fly. The soul bird trusts the air. Invisible forces hold it. It feels the Oneness, the unity with all. It remembers *I am loved.* It knows *I am loveable.* As we forget about the Unconditioned Self, we sense a basic doubt, or mistrust. The basic doubt arises from our perceived separateness. We wonder *Am I loved?* We fear *I am not loveable.*

Basic trust is essential in early childhood. In his classic text *Childhood and Society*, Erik Erikson identified eight stages of psychosocial development, each building upon the healthy completion of earlier stages. The first stage, Basic Trust versus Basic Mistrust, occurs between birth and age two. Basic trust is encouraged by, and reinforced by, loving and attentive mother and father figures. Mistrust arises from consistently unloving or inattentive parental figures. Unresolved, mistrust can lead later to an *identity crisis*, a term first coined by Erikson.

As D. W. Winnicott, the English psychologist and pediatrician who pioneered attachment theory in childhood development, writes, "At the start [a baby] absolutely needs to live in a circle of love and strength." Winnicott recognized that basic trust and a secure holding environment are essential for a child to experience what he called "a sense of being." This sense of being is an experience of aliveness that is primary in what Winnicott termed the True Self (that is, the Unconditioned Self). Without this support, a False Self replaces the True Self and acts as a mask of behavior, a defense against an environment that feels unsafe and unloving.

Spiritual teacher A. H. Almaas has written extensively about the "healing properties" of basic trust in both childhood and adulthood. He describes basic trust as a feeling of being "supported by reality." He says that basic trust teaches us that "life is fundamentally benevolent" and helps us to let go of the false images, identifications, beliefs, and ideas that cause us to feel unloveable and unworthy. He regards basic trust as faith in an "optimizing force" that helps us to engage in life and to be "courageous and authentic."

In his book *Facets of Unity*, Almaas writes:

> If we really have this trust, this deep inner relaxation, it becomes possible to live our lives out of love, out of an appreciation of life, out of enjoyment in what the universe provides for us, and out of compassion and kindness for others and ourselves. Without it, we live our lives defensively, in conflict with others and with ourselves, becoming self-centered and egoistic. To find our basic trust is to reconnect with our natural state that we have become separated from.

"I like the sound of basic trust," says Louise as she listens to me talk about it.

"Me, too," I tell her.

"Do you think this basic trust exists in all of us?" she asks.

"Yes."

"Where does this trust come from?"

"From the Oneness, which is our home," I reply.

"What happens to the basic trust?"

"Nothing, really," I say. "It's never really broken. It's always with us, but our perception obscures it."

"Like clouds covering up the sun," says Louise.

"Practicing gratitude is one way to make the sun come out again," I suggest.

"Gratitude helped me to say 'yes' again to my life," Louise says.

"Gratitude helps us to trust again," I add.

"From the One Infinite Intelligence comes everything we need," continues Louise. "All the guidance, all the healing, and all the help. And for that I am most grateful."

"Amen," I say.

Gift of Everything

My start date for writing this book was January 21. I had put this date in my calendar back in October. That gave me the necessary time to create a space in my schedule so I could write without distraction. Just a few days before I was due to start, something unexpected happened. I woke up with a pain in my butt. My left buttock felt sore. The nerve down my left leg was stiff. I tried to carry on as normal, but I couldn't. I had a consultation with a physiotherapist and also two sessions with a chiropractor. I tried to make the pain go away, but it got worse.

By the time I sat down to write, I was in a lot of physical pain. The muscles in my left buttock were knotted and bruised. A line of fire ran up and down the sciatic nerve in my left leg. My body was in a constant light sweat. I carried my body around like it was a wounded animal. I was afraid I wouldn't be able to write. My deadline didn't allow for any delay. Fortunately, the pain eased as I wrote. Sitting on a pile of soft cushions helped. I booked a few more sessions with my physiotherapist and with a craniosacral chiropractor. I really needed the pain to go way, but it kept getting worse.

Why now? I wondered. I was in good physical health. I hadn't fallen out of bed. I hadn't gotten stuck in a yoga pose. I absolutely had to write the book now, so the timing of my injury was inconvenient and significant. I tried to ignore it, but it wanted my attention. I prayed for it to go away, but it was still there. Eventually, it occurred to me that this injury wasn't an interruption in my schedule; it *was* my schedule. I needed to treat it with a more healing attitude. Who better to talk to then than Louise Hay?

Two days later, Louise and I talked on Skype. I told her about the sciatica. She agreed that the timing was significant. "Every book I write is a healing journey," she told me. That's true for me, too. All my books have taken me on journeys that never went according to plan. Not according to my conscious plan, anyway. Often I had to get lost in order to find my way. On every journey I found unexpected treasures and happiness.

"Well, how do you feel about having sciatica?" Louise asked me.

"I don't want it, and I don't like it," I told her.

"So, you want it to go away," she said.

"Yes."

"Are you afraid?" she asked.

"Yes."

"What are you afraid of?"

"I'm afraid I'll put on weight because I can't exercise," I said. "Not very deep, I know, but it's the first thing that comes to mind!"

"Don't judge the fear," she told me.

"Thank you," I said, grateful for the coaching.

"What else are you afraid of?" Louise asked.

"I'm afraid that it will last forever."

"You're afraid of feeling trapped," she said.

"Yes."

"Okay. The first thing you need to do is to dissolve this fear," she said.

"How do I do that?" I asked.

"With love," she said.

My attitude had been full of judgment. I treated the sciatica like it was a problem. I felt as if something was wrong with me. The timing was bad. I was rejecting the experience. I wasn't open. I was busy. And I was afraid. And I collected a few more fears along the way. When I told a friend about my sciatica, he told me that his dad had had to stop working because of sciatica. Another friend told me that his girlfriend had had sciatica ever since she was a teenager and that nothing could heal it.

Louise encouraged me to change my attitude toward the sciatica. "Let's not make this into a problem," she said. "Let's affirm that out of this situation only good will come." With the help of Louise's wise counsel, I suspended judgment. I started to treat the sciatica as an experience, not a problem. I decided not to resist the sciatica but to work in cooperation with it, and very quickly, I noticed I was less afraid. The pain began to ease, too. Over the next couple of weeks, I went from 100 percent pain, to 90 percent pain, to 75 percent pain.

Louise also encouraged me to choose my words carefully when speaking about sciatica. "Every cell of your body responds to what you think and what you say," she told me. Negative affirmations can spread like a virus when you are ill or unhappy. "How are you?" your friends ask. "I'm not well," you affirm. "I'm in pain," you tell them. Soon, all your friends know what's wrong, and then they make regular calls for updates. "I'm still ill," you affirm. "The pain is worse today," you tell them. Suddenly you're sending out hundreds of these mental tweets a day, and your body is reading them all.

In her book *Heart Thoughts*, Louise writes, "The body, like everything else in life, is a mirror of your inner thoughts and beliefs." She teaches us that a healing attitude is about being receptive to the messages of the body. "Pain is often a sign that you are not listening to a message," Louise told me. "Therefore, start by affirming, *I am willing to get the message.* Pay attention and let your body speak to you. Apologize for ignoring your body and tell it you are all ears now. Be grateful that your body is trying to tell you something. Your body isn't trying to make things difficult for you; it's trying to help you. Your body isn't against you; it's showing you how to love yourself and how to let life love you."

A few weeks ago, while aboard a flight to San Diego to see Louise, I read *When Things Fall Apart* by Pema Chödrön, a Tibetan Buddhist teacher. She quotes one of her students, who said, "'Buddha nature, cleverly disguised as fear, kicks our ass into being receptive.'" This message seemed somewhat apt for my posterior (notice how I didn't use the word *pain*) and me. During that visit with Louise, she encouraged me to listen for the message from the sciatica. We had some big conversations about releasing old pain, forgiving old wounds, living in the present, being more receptive, and, of course, letting life love me.

Slowly but surely, I have been befriending my sciatica. One morning, during a meditation, a question popped into my mind: *How would I behave if I was not afraid of this sciatica?* Contemplating this question eased the inflammation in my nervous system. My body felt more comfortable. The sensation levels dropped again to 60 percent, and then to 50 percent, and then to 45 percent. I was less afraid now and more open to guidance and inspiration.

"The first thing I want you to do every morning is to thank your body for all that it is doing to heal itself," Louise told me.

"Sorry, I can't do that," I said.

"Why not?" she asked.

"Well, the first thing I do every morning is thank my bed for a good night's sleep," I told her.

"Who taught you that?" she asked, laughing.

"Someone I love and respect very much."

"Well, she sounds very wise to me," said Louise with a smile.

"She is," I said.

"Always remember that your body wants to heal. And when you thank your body for all that it's doing, it really helps your body to heal," she said.

Louise prescribed one of her favorite affirmations for me. It is *I listen with love to my body's messages.* I took this affirmation into my daily meditation. Soon enough, a new plan of action appeared. I felt guided to have a series of sessions with my good friend Raina Nahar, a Reiki master and healer in London. My physiotherapist encouraged me to take up Pilates. I ordered a reformer, a scary-looking but very effective resistance-exercise machine for classic Pilates training. It arrived a few days later. I also followed two leads, given to me by friends, and met a local osteopath, Finn Thomas, and a new physiotherapist, Alan Watson: both helped me make significant breakthroughs in healing the sciatica.

Even with this new schedule and all the appointments and discomfort, I was still able to write this book, meeting each deadline on time along the way. As I write these words, the sensations in my sciatic nerve have continued to ease. I still have some messages I need to pay attention to. Writing *Life Loves You* has helped me love myself in a new way. It has also helped me be more open and receptive to letting life love me. It's a journey I'm grateful to be on.

Path of Trust

"I didn't have a healing attitude when I was first diagnosed with cancer," Louise tells me.

"What was your attitude?" I ask her.

"I was very afraid."

"What were you afraid of?"

"Cancer was a death sentence 40 years ago," she says.

"So you were afraid of dying?"

"Yes. I was also full of superstition."

"What do you mean?"

"Well, I believed cancer was a sign I was a bad person and that I'd got life all wrong," she says.

"How did you change your attitude?"

"I got a lot of help along the way."

"None of us are healed alone," I tell her.

"The willingness to heal was the real miracle," she says.

"How so?"

"When I was ready to do whatever it took to heal, I seemed to be led to exactly the right people."

"Can you give me an example?"

"In *You Can Heal Your Life*, I tell the story of how after learning about foot reflexology, I wanted to find a practitioner. That night, I attended a local lecture series. Usually I sat at the front, but this time I felt compelled to sit at the back. I didn't want to do this, but something inside me made me do it. Anyway, as soon as I sat down, a man came and sat next to me. He was a reflexologist, and he did home visits. So I booked him up!"

"That's beautiful," I say.

"As if by chance," she continues, "wonderful books would land on my lap, I'd hear about lectures in my neighborhood, and I'd meet all sorts of interesting people."

"You were being led on a path."

"Yes. It was a path of trust, and everything fell into place for me."

"What do you believe was leading you on this path?"

"My inner ding," Louise says, pointing to her chest.

"Thank God for the inner ding," I say, smiling.

"I quickly learned to trust my inner ding because of all the little miracles and coincidences that were happening to me," she tells me.

"It sounds like the big plan was taking care of you."

"Yes. And after six months, my doctors confirmed I was in remission. I knew, without any doubt, that the cancer was gone from my mind and my body."

In 1999, I wrote a book about personal growth and evolution called *Shift Happens!* In it I explored the power of trust and how trust can carry us through the worst of times and the best of times. Listening to Louise tell her story, I was reminded how trust can transform a mind-set of fear into love and how a path of trust can take us on profound and wonderful healing journeys. A couple of years after I wrote *Shift Happens!* I received an e-mail from a reader named Jenna, who told me about her own healing journey. Here's what she wrote:

Dear Dr. Holden,

I am a 42-year-old woman, living in New York City. A few months back (it feels like years ago now) I was diagnosed with breast cancer. My world stopped. I found myself in hell all of a sudden. It's been a long journey. So many people along the way have helped me. There have been miracles. Many miracles. One of them was finding your book on an empty seat on a subway train one day.

I remember when I picked up your book a voice in my head said, "This is a gift for you." I took one look at the title, and I smiled. The title was perfect. The title summed up how I felt about my life. "This is exactly what I need right now," I said to myself. I read and reread your book over the next few weeks. I kept it in my handbag. It sat on my bedside table. I took it to my doctor's appointments. Your book was my companion. It has been a friend to me.

Yesterday, I received the all-clear from my doctor. I am well again, but in a different way. Now I am well in my soul, not just in my body. This whole experience has helped me to see everything differently. I mean *everything* differently—even the title of your book. You see, I thought I was reading a book called *Shit Happens!* The title was perfect! Every day, ten times a day at least, I picked up *Shit Happens!* and read another chapter. I even recommended *Shit Happens!* to all my friends.

It was only yesterday, while sitting on the subway on my way home from the doctor, when I got out *Shit Happens!* again, that I saw for the first time what the real title of your book is.

I like this new title! The title is perfect. It sums up how I feel about my life.

Thank you,

Jenna

"When you are afraid, it is a sure sign that you are trusting in your own ego," I wrote in *Shift Happens!* (spelled with an *f*). The ego, which is your sense of a separate self, struggles to understand trust because trust is felt only in alignment with your soul. In *Shift Happens!* I wrote,

To the ego, trust feels like walking the plank. It is a death march. This is because trust takes you past your ego's perceptions to a field of greater possibilities. Trust invokes the highest in you. It gives you access to the unlimited potential of your Unconditioned Self. With trust, all things are possible.

Trust is not just positive thinking, it is a way of being. In its highest expression, it is a quality of awareness that belongs to your Unconditioned Self. Trust shows you that when your life is falling apart, it isn't *you* that's falling apart. The essence of who you are is always okay. What falls apart is your sense of self, your ego, and its plans, hopes, and expectations of how things should be. "Lives fall apart when they need to be rebuilt," writes Iyanla Vanzant, in *Peace from Broken Pieces*.

As I was preparing to write this chapter, I got news that my dear friend Sue Boyd had been admitted to Bristol Hospital. She was in a coma, diagnosed with encephalitis and unlikely to live. Doctors told us that if by some miracle Sue did regain consciousness, she would suffer severe brain damage. Sue's friends immediately set up a prayer circle. After a few days, we heard that Sue was awake. I made the journey to Bristol Hospital as soon as I could. I felt a wave of hesitation when I got to her ward. I was afraid that I might find Sue in terrible condition. I needn't have worried, though.

Sue was sitting up in bed. Two nurses were by her side, and she was making them laugh about something. "Bloody hell, old boy, it's so good to see you," she said, smiling when she noticed me. Sue and I have known each other for 20 years. She is love on legs. Everyone who knows her would agree with this description. She's a soul friend. We've shared much of our spiritual journeys together. While I was with Sue that day, I saw her take her first faltering steps with the help of her nurses. "These don't feel like my legs," she told them.

I listened to Sue's story of what happened. "What a big surprise!" she said. "I didn't think something like this would ever happen to me." Later on, she told me most emphatically, "I trust that there is a higher plan, with benefits, and I am fully signed up for it." When I mentioned how brave I thought she was, she said, "It's not really bravery, it's trust. All I can do is trust." During our conversation, I shared something that the spiritual teacher Ram Dass once said when we were talking about trust:

> Trust is the awareness that
> who you think you are cannot handle your life,
> but who you really are can and will.

I told Sue that I was about to write a chapter on gratitude that would include something about trust. Before I left, I gave her one of Louise Hay's Wisdom Cards. The message on it reads, *I trust the intelligence within me.* Sue smiled when she saw it. "Love is all that really matters," she said with 24 EEG electrodes stuck to her head. "You already knew that, Sue," I told her. The EEG monitor registered Sue's jolly laugh. "Yes, that's true," she said, "but I really know it now." I could tell from the look in Sue's eyes that she'd experienced something big. "I know what it's like to be me without a body," she told me, "and I tell you, it's all love."

The Holy Now

In our household, Bo and Christopher are the first to wake up in the morning. They don't wait till sunrise, they don't need an alarm clock, and they're always raring to go. Hollie and I are usually bounced out of our peaceful sleep by two little bodies crawling all over our bed.

"Wake up, Dad!" shouts Bo.

"Come on, Dad!" shouts Christopher.

"Dad, Dad," shouts Bo, tugging at my nightshirt.

"Let's go downstairs," shouts Christopher.

"Good morning, people," I say, barely able to breathe.

"It's the day!" says Bo, more softly now that she sees I'm regaining consciousness.

"Let's play trains," shouts Christopher.

"What time is it?" I ask, because it feels like 3:00 A.M.

"It's wake-up time," says Bo.

"Yeah. Come on, Dad," says Christopher, who can't even tell time.

"Have you thanked your bed for a good night's sleep?" I ask, trying to buy a few more precious seconds.

"Yes," says Bo.

"Yes," shouts Christopher.

"Let's go!" says Bo.

"Now!" shouts Christopher.

Now is very holy to children. There's no other time quite like it. Now is the natural dwelling place for them. They don't spend much time in the past or the future. Now is always a brand-new adventure. Adults often interpret children's steadfast focus on now as a sign of impatience or even rudeness, but really it's a sign of aliveness. Now is the only real time. And now is the time for the fun to start.

Christopher and Bo usually target me first thing in the morning and leave Hollie alone to sleep. My theory is that Hollie is awake, but she knows how to lie still. She'll probably have something to say about this theory when she reads it. I have proof of it, though. When Christopher and Bo are trying to wake me up, they sometimes say something very funny, and I can hear Hollie's silent laughter. The slight change in her breathing is what gives her away. Like the time when I asked Bo and Christopher for another five minutes.

"Good morning, Dad," shouted Bo, ruffling my hair.

"Wake up, Dad," shouted Christopher, leaning on my chest.

"It's the day," shouted Bo.

"Now, Dad!" shouted Christopher.

"What time is it?" I asked

"The clock says 5 and 5 and 5," said Bo, meaning 5:55 A.M.

"Yeah," said Christopher.

"Okay, give me five more minutes," I told them.

"Bo, what's five minutes?" asked Christopher.

"I don't know, but it's important to Daddy," Bo told him.

Children have a huge faith in now. Now means more to them than the past or the future. Now is their best chance for happiness. Now is where they will find love. Now is the time to go for it. When they look into now, they see the totality of possibilities that Louise speaks of. Now is their mirror. Early on, children are still aligned with the basic truth *I am loveable.* This basic truth gives rise to the basic trust that *I am loved.* Now is a good time. Now is a time of innocence.

When we lose faith in ourselves, we stop trusting in the present moment to care for us and give us what we need. The basic fear *I am not loveable* and the basic doubt *Am I loved?* distort our perception. We project our forgetfulness onto the present moment. Hence, we judge that this moment is not good enough. It looks like something is missing. Now doesn't feel real to us anymore, and so we either try to retrace our steps back to the past or we journey toward a better future. But without now, we are lost.

"Like the Prodigal Son, we all eventually return to NOW to find our spiritual home," I wrote in *Shift Happens!* This journey back to now is a healing journey. It takes a lot of courage because as we start to come back to now, we face all our self-judgment, our self-criticism, our self-rejection, and our perceived loss of innocence. "The present moment is a pretty vulnerable place," writes Pema Chödrön in *When Things Fall Apart*. Yet it's only when we come back again to the mirror of now that we can remember what is real and let go of what is not true.

A great gift in my life is my occasional correspondence with the poet Daniel Ladinsky. Daniel and I have e-mailed each other since I first came across his renderings of the Sufi poet Hafiz some 15 years ago. I've featured Daniel's translations of Hafiz in several of my works, especially *Loveability*. In *The Subject Tonight Is Love: 60 Wild and Sweet Poems of Hafiz*, Daniel includes a poem I knew I'd feature in this book at some point. Called *This Place Where You Are Right Now*, it's about basic trust—an homage to now. Here's how the poem begins:

> This place where you are right now
> God circled on a map for you.
>
> Wherever your eyes and arms and heart can move
> Against the earth and sky,
> The Beloved has bowed there—
>
> Our beloved has bowed there knowing
> You were coming.

Basic trust recognizes that you are loveable and that life loves you now. Now offers you salvation and enlightenment, regardless of your trespasses or your terrible history. Now is another name for love. Now is another name for God. Louise Hay has a huge faith in now. You could say she has the faith of a child. "I healed my life by changing my relationship to now," she once told me. The gift of now is that we always have a chance to start over. Every now is an invitation to let go of the past. Every now is a ticket to a better future. Every now has a gift for us, if only we'd look again.

Basic trust encourages you to see that you have the best seat in the house for your life journey. Wherever you are right now—in your job, your marriage, your financial status, your physical well-being, your emotional history, the prison you're in—might not be where you want to end up, but it is the perfect place to start your healing journey. "Whatever the present moment contains, accept it as if you had chosen it," writes Eckhart Tolle in *The Power of Now*. "Always work with it, not against it. Make it your friend and ally, not your enemy. This will miraculously transform your whole life."

In my book *Happiness NOW!*, I observed that the best chance for healing and happiness is always in the present moment. To be truly happy we have to be willing to give up the search for happiness and look again right here. I also shared the following line of letters:

HAPPINESSISNOWHERE

There are at least two ways to read these letters, as I wrote in *Happiness NOW!* "The difference between 'happiness is nowhere' and 'happiness is now here' has something to do with the event, and everything to do with how you *see* the event. Your perception is key."

Without basic trust, you use each present moment as a stepping-stone to get to somewhere else. You pursue happiness, chase success, and search for love, but you never find them where you are. "In my healing journey I made a conscious choice to live more in the present," Louise once told me. "At first, it was like moving into an empty house—cold and impersonal. But the more I lived in the present, the more I began to feel at home. Living in the present is how I learned to trust life and to see that everything I need is here for me."

In every single moment there is a lesson, there is a gift, there is a teaching, and there is a message—all for you. What is the purpose of all this help? What is all this cosmic love for? Well, I think Louise sums it up beautifully in an affirmation from her book *Power Thoughts: 365 Daily Affirmations*. The affirmation is:

Every moment presents a wonderful new opportunity to become more of who I am.

PRACTICE 5:
DAILY GRATITUDE

"Guess what I do last thing at night?" says Louise, with a twinkle in her eye.

"What do you do?" I ask.

"I go to bed with thousands of people all over the world," she says, laughing.

"How do you do that?"

"People take me to bed with them!" she says.

"How lovely!"

"They download me so that we can lie in bed and meditate together before going to sleep," she explains.

"Louise Hay, you are full of mischief!"

"Guess what else I do before I go to sleep?"

"I can't imagine," I say.

"I go through my day, blessing and being grateful for each experience," she tells me.

"Do you do this in bed?"

"Yes, mostly. The other night I opened up my pocket mirror—the one you gave me with the inscription *Life Loves You*—and I said my gratitudes out loud to the mirror," she tells me.

"Saying gratitudes out loud is very powerful," I say.

"Yes, it's much more powerful than just thinking about them," says Louise.

"I love sharing gratitudes with my daughter, Bo, as she falls asleep at night."

"Encouraging children to practice gratitude is so important," says Louise.

"It's also a lot of fun."

"If you start the day with gratitude and end the day with gratitude, your life will be filled with blessings that you couldn't see before," says Louise.

"You can't know how powerful gratitude is until you start to practice it," I say.

"Practicing gratitude is always better than you can imagine," says Louise.

"You have to do it in order to experience the miracle," I say.

"Gratitude is a miracle," says Louise.

Gratitude is a spiritual practice. Every time you give thanks for your life, even if it's only for green lights and free parking spaces, you take a step closer to love. Gratitude always takes you in the direction of love. Gratitude takes you to your heart. Practicing gratitude helps you to cultivate a loving awareness for your life and for yourself. When you remember to give thanks you feel blessed, not just for what you have but also for who you are. Practicing gratitude helps you to remember the basic truth *I am loveable*. The more you practice gratitude, the more you become who you really are.

Gratitude is a training in vision. Imagine you're looking into a mirror and you're about to say out loud ten things you're grateful for in your life at present. Chances are, if you've not done a gratitude exercise like this before, you might struggle at first. You might even tell yourself that it's impossible to name ten things. If, however, you pay attention to your life and stay close to your heart, you will find ten quite easily. In fact, you will usually find more than ten. Gratitude brings a new awareness. It transforms your psychology. It opens your eyes. You see the world differently.

Gratitude is a Sacred Yes. When gratitude is easy, it's a sign that you're on track with your life; when gratitude is difficult, however, it's a sign that you need to stop, because you've wandered away from yourself and forgotten what is truly sacred. Practicing gratitude helps you to identify and appreciate the Sacred Yesses in your life. When you begin the day with gratitude, as Louise does, you won't get lost. Gratitude is a prayer that helps you to stay on track and say yes to what is real. E.E. Cummings wrote a beautiful poem that begins:

> i thank You God for most this amazing
> day:for the leaping greenly spirits of trees
> and a blue dream of sky;and for everything
> which is natural which is infinite which is yes

Gratitude expands your awareness. When I told Louise about my sciatica, she talked about the healing power of gratitude. "At some point you'll be grateful for this sciatica," she said. "I'm not saying that you should be grateful for it now. It might be too soon. But at some point, you will be grateful because you'll see that this sciatica has a message or even a gift for you." After Louise told me this, I did an inquiry in which I completed this statement ten times: *I am grateful for this sciatica because* . . . I found this practice so enlightening and helpful. The sensations in my sciatic nerve soon calmed down to 30 percent and then to 20 percent.

Gratitude supports basic trust. Gratitude helps you to suspend your judgment. It gives you another angle, another way of looking at things. "Life doesn't happen *to* you, it happens *for* you," I wrote in *Be Happy*. Sometimes cancellations, rejections, traffic delays, bad weather, and even more bad weather can come bearing gifts. A layoff, an illness, or the end of a relationship may well be the start of something wonderful. "We don't know what anything is really for," says Louise. "Even a tragedy might turn out to be for our greatest good. That's why I like to affirm *Every experience in my life benefits me in some way.*"

Gratitude brings you back to now. Practicing gratitude helps you to be more present in your life. The more present you are, the less you feel like something is missing. Recently somebody posted this message on my Facebook page: "You may think the grass is greener on the other side, but if you take the time to water your own grass it will be just as green." Practicing gratitude helps you to water your own grass. Gratitude helps you to make the most of everything as it happens. Gratitude teaches you that happiness is always now.

Our spiritual practice for you in this chapter is called *Daily Gratitude*. We invite you to stand in front of a mirror and complete the following sentence ten times: *One thing I am grateful for in my life right now is . . .*

Please make sure you do this exercise out loud. Hearing yourself say your gratitudes doubles the effect. We encourage you to do this vocal gratitude exercise once in the morning and once at night for seven days. Remember, these spiritual practices don't work in theory, only in practice. By practicing gratitude now, you step into your life in a whole new way. Gratitude takes you by the hand, and you see even more clearly that you are loveable and that life loves you.

CHAPTER 6

Learning to Receive

There are so many gifts
Still unopened from your birthday.

HAFIZ

While we were writing *Life Loves You*, Louise Hay, at the age of 87, held her first public art exhibition. The ArtBeat on Main Street Gallery in downtown Vista, California, hosted the exhibit. It was called *The Art of Louise Hay* and featured 20 of Louise's oil and watercolor paintings. Louise attended the gallery reception, held on January 25, and people traveled near and far to see her work. I phoned her the day before the reception to congratulate her. "I feel very blessed," she told me.

Blessing Buddha is Louise's portrait of the Buddha. It was the centerpiece of her exhibit. A magnificent oil painting, it stands three feet tall and two-and-a-half feet wide. A golden Buddha, dressed in saffron and royal blue, sits in lotus posture upon a lotus throne, which is painted fuchsia and pink. A halo of white light surrounds the Buddha's head. He holds a jar in his left hand, as in portraits of the Medicine Buddha. Layered brushstrokes of emerald green, yellow, and more saffron fill in the background.

Blessing Buddha now hangs in the lobby of Hay House headquarters in Carlsbad, California. "It welcomes and blesses all who enter," says Louise. I love the painting. I have a full-sized copy hanging by the door to my office at home. I look at it and receive a blessing every day as I commute up the stairs to work. Louise has not written or spoken about the Buddha in any of her major works. I was keen, therefore, to learn what she thinks about the Buddha and also to explore any relationship between the Blessing Buddha and her philosophy that life loves you.

"The Buddha is a living saint," Louise tells me. "I believe he had an experience of the Unconditioned

Self, as you call it. In his awakening, he experienced the One Infinite Mind, and he received the blessings of creation." I ask Louise to tell me more about this. She says, "We are created by a Universal Consciousness that supports all of its creations. We are the beloved children of the Universe and we have been given everything. We are born blessed. The message the Buddha has for each and every one of us is *I am blessed*."

"How long did it take you to paint *Blessing Buddha*?" I ask Louise.

"Eighty-five years!" she says with a big laugh.

"Good answer."

"It took about five years in total," she says.

"That was a long journey."

"It was a journey I couldn't have taken alone," she says.

"What do you mean?"

"I had two wonderful art teachers who stretched me far beyond what I thought I was capable of doing."

Louise's first teacher was an English artist who occasionally visited San Diego. "I took his class when he was in town, and he gave me the assignment of drawing the Buddha," she told me. Louise hadn't done anything like that before. "Drawing the Buddha took great precision. It was like taking a class in mathematics. I had to erase a lot of lines," she said with a big smile. "It was my teacher's idea that I draw the Buddha, and I couldn't have done it without his gentle encouragement."

Louise finished drawing the Buddha after many sessions and then set about painting the figure. "I started to paint it by myself, but I wasn't happy with it," she said, so she set the drawing aside. It sat on an easel in her painting room for a couple of years. "One day I remember thinking, *When the student is ready, the teacher appears*," Louise recalled. "Shortly after that I met my next teacher, Linda Bounds." Louise formed a close friendship with Linda, a local artist. "Linda brought out artistic abilities in me that I didn't know I possessed," Louise told me. "We took a journey together that I will treasure forever."

Linda taught Louise to paint by brushing layer upon layer of color onto the canvas. Painting *Blessing Buddha* took about two years. It was during this time that the painting became a meditation for Louise. She began to tune in to the life of the Buddha. She was struck by what she called "a universal benevolence" that moved through him, and this gave her the idea to name her painting *Blessing Buddha*.

"I began to have a conversation with the Buddha," Louise told me.

"What did you talk about?" I asked.

"Everything," she said with a smile.

"Be specific," I said.

"I asked the Buddha to help me with my painting," she said.

"Wise move."

"I told the Buddha I was afraid I couldn't do the painting," she added.

"What did the Buddha say?"

"He said, 'Remember that the Universe loves you and wants you to succeed at everything you do.'"

Each time Louise worked on the painting, she tuned in more to the Buddha's experience of enlightenment. "First I asked the Buddha to help me paint the Buddha. He was very helpful with that, and so I started to ask for help with other things. I asked for support with loving myself more, forgiving others, being grateful, and being open to guidance. I didn't ask the Buddha for material things; I asked for help with my mind. I see the Buddha as very compassionate and as a universal friend who is here to help us all."

When I asked Louise to sum up her experience of painting *Blessing Buddha*, she said, "*Blessing Buddha* taught me to be very patient with myself and also very kind. To paint this picture I had to find the little-girl me—the girl I call Lulu—who paints without any fear or self-criticism or self-doubt. Above all, I had to be more open and more willing to receive. This painting was done through me, not by me. That's why the full name for my painting is *Blessing Buddha: Ask and You Shall Receive.*"

The Already Principle

"I remember when I first discovered I was truly prosperous," Louise tells me.

"When was that?" I ask.

"It was when I realized I could afford to buy any book I wanted," she says.

"How old were you?"

"I was in my mid-40s or so," she says.

"Why books?"

"I had very little money. I didn't even own a watch. Books felt like a luxury, but they were affordable," she tells me.

"What were you reading?"

"Florence Scovel Shinn's book *The Game of Life and How to Play It* was a big inspiration. I liked her practical, no-nonsense approach," says Louise.

"You and Florence could easily be soul sisters," I tell her.

"I've always felt a strong kinship with her," Louise says, smiling.

"What else did you read?"

"Emmet Fox's works were a big help," she says.

"Why did these books help you feel prosperous?"

"They spoke of an innate potential for love and prosperity that exists in all of us," she says.

"How did you feel about that?"

"Well, at first I thought it was ridiculous!" she says with a big laugh.

"Why?"

"The abundance of the universe had nothing to do with me. I could believe it existed for others, but not for me."

"You didn't feel loveable," I say.

"I had very poor self-esteem back then. I was also very angry," she says.

"Why were you angry?"

"These books told me that I was the one who was blocking my potential for love and prosperity," she says, laughing again.

"Yet still you kept turning the pages."

"Yes. These books were my lifelines. I remember

telling myself that now that I'd found these books I would find a way to experience this potential for love and prosperity, and that I wouldn't let myself forget about this potential ever again," she says.

I reflect on Louise's story about when she first felt truly prosperous. Those books were her Aladdin's lamps. They woke up a potential that already existed in her. This potential was waiting for her to take the first step on her healing journey. And here she is now, some 40 years later, one of the best-selling authors on the planet.

"When did you first feel truly prosperous?" Louise asks me.

"When I was 18 years old," I tell her.

"You were very young," says Louise.

"I elected to take my midlife crisis early," I say.

"We shouldn't compare our journeys, I know, but sometimes I wish I'd learned what I know now a lot sooner," she says.

"'There is a Divine Design for each man!'" I say, quoting Florence Scovel Shinn, which makes Louise smile.

"So what happened when you were 18 years old?" she asks.

"I met Avanti Kumar, my first spiritual mentor."

"What did he tell you?"

"Well, he gave me a lot of books to read. Books like the *Tao Te Ching*, the *Bhagavad Gita*, *The Dhammapada*, and *Autobiography of a Yogi*, which is where I first learned about affirmations. These books were my lifelines."

"Did you struggle like I did?" she asks.

"Yes. Just like you, I believed in a divine potential that exists in everyone else but not in me," I tell her.

"You felt unloveable," she says.

"Yes, but I kept on turning the pages."

"You were listening to your inner ding," Louise says with a smile.

"I'm so grateful that I did."

"So how did this help you feel prosperous?" she asks.

"Avanti was the first person to tell me that I am already abundant," I tell her.

"Did you believe him?" she asks.

"I asked Avanti, 'If I'm already abundant, why can't I feel it?' And he said it was because I was blocking it!"

"I hope you got angry," Louise says, laughing.

"Yeah, I did some pillow bashing," I tell her.

"And then what?"

"Avanti said something that blew my socks off!"

"What did he say?"

"He said the reason I didn't feel abundant already is that I didn't expect to feel abundant now; I expected to feel abundant in the future."

"That's very good," says Louise.

"Avanti helped me take my first step on the spiritual path."

"What was that first step?" asks Louise.

"It was the willingness to seek the blocks to love inside myself."

"Dissolving our barriers," says Louise.

"Amen."

Avanti Kumar taught me what I call *The Already Principle*. The Unconditioned Self, which is our true nature, is already blessed. "From the very beginning, all beings are Buddha," said Hakuin, a Japanese Zen Master. We carry with us a timeless wisdom that exists already in us and helps us to remember what we forgot. In the depths of our soul, we find our divine inheritance. We discover that we already are the person we most want to be.

Divine potential exists now, not in the future. This potential is our divine mirror. We see our God-given talents in this mirror. This is where we find the big happiness, the timeless wisdom, and the boundless love. Somehow, though, we forget about this mirror. It gets covered over with a thousand Post-it notes. These notes have terrible messages written on them, like *I'm not loveable* and *I'm not enough*. They are full of our judgments and self-criticism, self-rejection and unworthiness. Pablo Picasso is often quoted as saying that "[e]very child is an artist. The problem is how to remain an artist once we grow up."

According to the Already Principle, you have already been given everything you need for your journey in this life. No matter which road you take, divine guidance will meet you there. "I am fully equipped for the Divine Plan of my life; I am more than equal to the situation," wrote Florence Scovel Shinn. Florence's affirmation reminds me of the scene in the film *Mary Poppins* in which, before Jane's and Michael's eyes, Mary Poppins pulls item after item from her bottomless carpetbag. Our real potential is like this. It reveals itself when it is needed and when we ask for it. It's bigger than anything our ego can carry.

What about our darkest moments, when our ego is on its knees? When we doubt that love exists? When we can see "only one set of footprints" and feel utterly alone? In terrible times, it's virtually impossible for anyone to say the right thing. Words are probably not appropriate, anyway. They make a wound sting even more. You can't possibly know it then, but even in the most forsaken place, the healing has already begun. That's how reality works. Nothing takes place outside the Oneness. Love abandons no one.

The Already Principle reminds us of our true nature and the nature of reality. It teaches us that there is more to this world than meets the eye. Even in a world of fear, there is love. Even when you are in lack, there is abundance. Even when you experience conflict, there is peace. Even when you are alone, there is help. Even when you are confused, there is guidance. Everything you need is here, and it's here now. That's why Louise always encourages us to pray and affirm in the present tense. Just like this:

I am willing to let life love me today.

Everything I need to know is revealed to me.

I gratefully accept all the good I have
in my life now.

I release all struggle now, and I am at peace.

My healing is already in progress.

I now accept and appreciate the
abundant life the Universe offers me.

Beyond Independence

I teach a module called "Life Loves You" in my three-day *Loveability* program. In this module, we explore the blocks to love. We look especially at the ways we make it difficult to be loved. We see how our lack of self-love makes it harder for others to love us. We examine fears about love, roles we play in relationships, old grievances we carry, and defenses that stop us from letting love in. One block to love we pay special attention to is independence.

How independent are you? I ask my students this question at the start of the "Life Loves You" module. I follow that question up with this one: *Are you a H.I.P. or a D.I.P.?* I explain that H.I.P. stands for Healthy Independent Person and D.I.P. stands for Dysfunctional Independent Person. On the spectrum of independence, there is a healthy range and a dysfunctional range. It's important that you know the difference and that you choose well, if you want to let life love you.

Healthy independence is a creative force that moves through everyone and everything. This creative force comes from the Oneness. It's how the Unified Field— the energy of the universe—grows flowers and whales, rainbows and stars, amethysts and people. It gives form to life and makes embryos into babies. It helps children take their first steps and stand on their own two feet. "I can do it all by myself," cries the child. Soon he can run and play. And all of this happens not in isolation but in a holding environment of support and love.

Healthy independence helps you to take your place in the collective. It helps you to express yourself as *I Am*. You know deep inside yourself that *I am blessed* and *I am loved* and *I am loveable*. You are an *I* that is made out of everything. Everything helped to create you. This isn't just poetry, by the way; this is science. In the "Life Loves You" module, I show my students a short film featuring Carl Sagan, the astrophysicist and cosmologist. In it Sagan says, "If you wish to make an apple pie from scratch, you must first invent the universe."

Healthy independence promotes freedom of thought. It helps you to know your own mind, which is, in its purest form, an expression of your Unconditioned Self. It helps you to be "independent of the good opinion of others," as the psychologist Abraham

Maslow explained in his work on the hierarchy of needs. Healthy independence helps you to be free of conditioning and to express yourself freely. It helps you to individuate, to become fully yourself, and to be the wise woman or wise man that you are.

"Healthy independence saved my life," Louise once told me. "It gave me the courage to leave home at 15 and to escape from abuse." Healthy independence can get you out of a bad situation. It helps you to rely on an innate wisdom that is your true power. It saves you from losing yourself in unhealthy dependency, giving up on yourself, or throwing yourself away. Without healthy independence, family patterns wouldn't be healed, and humanity could not evolve in the direction of love.

So what about dysfunctional independence? In basic terms, dysfunctional independence is a mistake. It takes a good thing too far. We stop relating to ourselves as an individual expression of the universe. Instead, we believe we are self-made. We exist in isolation. This is how the eyes of the body see it. However, when you look through the eyes of the heart, or through the lens of quantum physics, you discover that all forms of separation, including a personal ego, are "an optical delusion," as Albert Einstein put it.

Dysfunctional independence is very lonely. It puts you outside of the Oneness in a place you could call hell. The problem with being a D.I.P. is that it separates you from everything, including yourself. As you lose conscious contact with others, you lose contact with yourself as well. Your sense of self breaks apart. When it gets really bad, you can't feel your heart, you are physically disembodied, your mind is at odds with itself, and you're not sure anymore if you have a soul. Your ego tries to be everything that the Unconditioned Self is, but without the support of that Self, it ends up feeling lonely, tired, and unloved.

Dysfunctional independence is very frightening. It's a choice we make out of fear, and it also causes a lot of fear. Most commonly, dysfunctional independence is a reaction to a wound. Once upon a time, you got hurt. You withdrew inside yourself and you felt safe. You decided to build a castle wall around yourself. The wall was designed to protect you from being hurt again. The wall did its job. It kept the world out. Unfortunately, this left you alone with your original wound. Nothing could get through to you: not help, not the people who love you, not even the angels.

Dysfunctional independence is a block to love. The more of a D.I.P. you become, the more closed off you are from everything. This should make you safe, according to your ego, but it doesn't. The more closed off you are, the more fearful you are of everything, including love. That's why it's so hard for anyone to love you. You fear that love will hurt you, and you don't want to get hurt again. The truth is, however, that love has never hurt you. It's only what is not love that hurts. Love can only ever love you, and it's only love that can save you.

Dysfunctional independence is the end of the road. You can go only so far by yourself. Being a D.I.P. blocks your growth. You are trying to do life by yourself, without feedback, without help, without love, and it's not working. "Individuality is only possible if it unfolds from wholeness," said physicist David Bohm. In other words, it's only when we go back to the Oneness—and when we let life love us—that we can fulfill our true destiny and be who we truly are.

Louise once told me, "All the doors of the universe are always open for you. The door to wisdom is open. The door to healing is open. The door to love is open. The door to forgiveness is open. The door to prosperity is open. This is true whether you are having a great day or not!" The Oneness is open at all hours. On the other side of dysfunctional independence is a universe of inspiration and love. Life is waiting for you. All you have to do is knock a hole in your wall, install a door, and start to let the love in.

Your Unconditioned Self, which rests in a state of basic openness, is always open to love. In the "Life Loves You" module, I share with my students one of Louise's favorite exercises on love. The idea is to stand in front of a mirror with arms open wide and say, "I am willing to let the love in. It is safe to let the love in. I say yes to letting love in." Louise recommends you do this three times a day. It's a very simple exercise that helps to open doors and, eventually, to bring down walls.

I end my "Life Loves You" module with a wonderful prayer by Louise on basic openness:

In the infinity of life where I am,
all is perfect, whole, and complete.

I believe in a power far greater than I am
that flows through me every moment of every day.

I open myself to the wisdom within,
knowing that there is only One Intelligence in this Universe.

Out of this One Intelligence comes all the answers,
all the solutions, all the healings, all the new creations.

I trust this Power and Intelligence,
knowing that whatever I need to know is revealed to me,
and that whatever I need comes to me
in the right time, space, and sequence.

All is well in my world.

Letting Go of Struggle

Even
After
All this time
The sun never says to the earth,

"You owe
Me."

Look
What happens
With a love like that,
It lights the
Whole
Sky.

This poem, *The Sun Never Says*, is another beautiful collaboration between Hafiz and Daniel Ladinsky. It gives us a glimpse of the unconditional nature of love. It reminds us that true love is freely given, at no cost, and that it is equally available to us all. This love is greater than anyone can conceive because it has no limits. No one can get his or her head around this love, so to speak. It's not just an idea. It comes from the Oneness. It is the original energy of the Unified Field. It is the basic consciousness of life. It is the heart of the universe expressing its boundless generosity.

Love is unconditional. This is easy to remember when we are aligned with our Unconditioned Self. Then we live with a natural awareness of the basic truth *I am loveable* and with the basic trust that *I am loved.* However, when we fall from grace for whatever reason, we lose sight of who we are and what love is. Love becomes a myth or, even worse, a religion. The basic fear that *I am not loveable* and the basic mistrust that *I am not loved* distorts our perception, and the ego turns love into its own image. Now love is separate from us. And we fear we must deserve love if we are ever to be loved again.

Love is never earned; it is freely given. To let love be love and to let life love you, you have to accept that love has nothing to do with deserving. Love is not a bargain. It is not a coin to be spent. Love will never say to you, "You owe me." Love is not a judgment. No matter how terrible your past may be, love waits for you. Love exempts no one. Not even you. Not even your worst enemy. The unconditional nature of love is what makes love so powerful. It dissolves every barrier. It undoes every block. It brings everyone home.

As long as you believe that love has to be deserved, you will place a limit on how much life can love you. Your self-image will set the conditions, not love. Your ego will write the contract, not love. This contract is an internal affair, full of personal rules and standards that love knows nothing about. The conditions of the contract vary from person to person. There are all sorts of clauses, such as *I can let life love me if . . .* and *I can let life love me when . . .* Three of the most common classifications of these clauses are the work ethic, the suffering ethic, and the martyr ethic.

"Life loves us, and life will help us to write this book," affirmed Louise in an e-mail on the day we agreed to do *Life Loves You*. In the same e-mail she wrote, "This book is already written. All we have to do is let it happen." Her words reminded me of a Buddhist monk I met in Bodh Gaya, India. We met by the

Bodhi Tree, also known as the Bo Tree, which grows next to the Mahabodhi Temple. It was at this spot—called the Immoveable Spot—that Siddhartha Gautama experienced enlightenment and became known as the Buddha—one who is awake.

The monk was working on an elaborate *thangka,* a painting on cotton and silk of the Vajradhara Buddha, who represents the essence of universal love and wisdom. When I commented on his beautiful artwork, the monk smiled and said, "I am God's photocopy machine. God gives me the images. All I do is faithfully copy the images onto the page." He told me that a true artist works with focus but not effort. "The effort comes not from ego but from the Great Determination in the sky," he said.

One reason I love to write is because every piece of writing is a co-creation and collaboration. Even though writing is a solitary act, an author never writes alone. On good days, the writing flows easily and without much effort. On difficult days, of which I've had a few, the writing doesn't flow. I can feel that the words are here, but they aren't lining up on the page. Usually the block is that I'm trying too hard. I'm trying to push the flow. I'm trying to make it happen, rather than letting it happen.

While writing this book I received many love notes from Louise encouraging me to work without effort, to be open to inspiration, to let myself be guided, and to trust the process. Just as she had done with *Blessing Buddha*, she wanted this work to come *through* us. Early on we created a list of affirmations to help us focus on our book. They included: *The life that loves us is writing this book; Everyday life helps us write* Life Loves You; and *We are grateful for all the support and guidance we receive in writing* Life Loves You. I make a list of affirmations for every book I write, and it was especially fun to do this with Louise.

Louise doesn't do work ethic. Not in the normal way, anyway. She doesn't believe in the adage *If you want something done properly, you have to do it yourself.* She doesn't subscribe to being an independent doer. "I struggled so much in the first half of my life, because I didn't know a better way," she told me. "I tried to do everything by myself, and I ended up divorced, unhappy, and with cancer. Gradually, as I let myself be helped and became more open to receiving, my life became less of a struggle. Over time I learned to love myself and to trust that life loves me too."

Louise is adamant that, in truth, there are no barriers to love. "The barriers we experience are imagined, not real," she says. They are dreamed up by our ego, not by love. "Life does not want us to suffer," she says. Mostly we suffer because we are unaware of the Divine Assistance available to us in each moment. We think we have to do it all by ourselves. We suffer, we struggle, and we live in sacrifice, because we let life love us only so much.

In Bodh Gaya many centuries ago, when Siddhartha sat beneath the Bodhi Tree, he was tired of searching for enlightenment. He wanted his enlightenment now. On his travels he had practiced asceticism, extreme sacrifice, and noble suffering in an effort to achieve enlightenment. He had not been successful. And then, as he sat upon the Immovable Spot, he decided to end his search. He stopped trying. He relaxed. He didn't do anything. In that moment he experienced the great blessings of the universe.

It is said that the Buddha's first words upon awakening were "I am now enlightened with all beings." This is hugely significant. He didn't say, "I am more enlightened than you." Or "I am enlightened and you are not." He experienced an enlightenment that exists, in potential, for all of us. And the potential exists now, not in the future. Love makes itself available to us when we make ourselves available to love. We are all in the Oneness. We are all part of love's great work.

Universal love, like the sun, shines on everyone. Love leaves no one out. As Galileo Galilei, the Italian physicist and philosopher, is said to have observed,

> The sun, with all those
> planets revolving around it
> and dependent upon it,
> can still ripen a bunch
> of grapes as if it had
> nothing else in
> the universe
> to do.

PRACTICE 6:
A RECEIVING JOURNAL

Louise and I are having breakfast in her kitchen. She brings over two smoothies that she has whipped up in her blender. "Here," she says, handing me a glass. The smoothie is thick, and it smells like a vegetable patch. "What's in this?" I ask. Louise smiles. "Everything that's good for you," she says. In other words, she's not going to tell me. "All you have to do is receive," she says. She knows that receiving is our topic of conversation this morning. Before taking my first sip I pray out loud, "Oh God, help me to receive."

While we drink our smoothies, Louise and I watch a short film of her art exhibition at the ArtBeat Gallery on her iPad. The exhibit was hugely popular. The original plan was for a two-week run. It was extended to six weeks. Hundreds of prints of *Blessing Buddha* were sold. Each one was signed by Louise and raised money for her charity, the Hay Foundation.

"I never expected to show my art," Louise tells me.

"Your art was a gift to yourself," I say.

"As a child, I wasn't encouraged to express my creativity," she says.

"Me neither."

"I was told I couldn't dance, so I stopped dancing," Louise says.

"I was put in the non-singing group in my class," I tell her.

"For years, I told myself 'I am not creative,'" she says.

"That's a powerful affirmation."

"The creativity of the universe flows through everyone," she affirms.

"No exceptions!"

"Everyone is creative, and we create our lives every day," she says.

"Our life is the real canvas," I suggest.

"Yes. And by tapping into the creative flow of the universe, we express our true potential, and we work miracles in our life," she says.

"How do we tap into this creativity?"

"By learning to receive," she replies.

Blessed are they who receive. Receiving, at the purest level, is about being open and receptive to your true nature. It's not about things; it's about you. It's not about having or getting; it's about being. To know who you are, without conditions or pretenses, requires genuine receptivity. It's about self-acceptance. *Who am I when I am not judging and rejecting myself?* This is your inquiry. Follow the open road, and it will take you back home to your Unconditioned Self. Here's where you experience the original blessing. It's like honey in your bones.

Receiving is a spiritual practice. Each time you affirm *I am open and receptive to my highest good,* you are cultivating a state of basic openness. In the Buddhist tradition, the word for basic openness is *shunyata*. It describes the awareness of your original mind that is empty of ego, fear, self-judgment, unworthiness, self-doubt, grievances, and complaining. Shunyata is what love feels like. This basic openness helps you to be receptive to beauty, inspiration, guidance, healing, and love.

Receiving is a great big Yes. "The universe says yes to you," says Louise. "It wants you to experience your highest good. When you ask for your highest good, the Universe doesn't say, 'I'll think about it'; it says yes. The universe is always saying yes to your highest good." And you have to say yes, too. The key to receiving is willingness, or readiness. When you declare, "I am ready to receive my highest good in this situation," it shifts your perception and your circumstances.

"When the student is ready, the teacher appears," Louise told herself, and shortly afterward her art teacher, Linda Bounds, appeared. "I said the same thing to myself when I wanted a really good local Pilates teacher," Louise told me. "And two days later I met Ahlea Khadro." Ahlea is the mother of Elliot, the little boy at our Thanksgiving lunch who kept going over to the mirror to smile at himself. Ahlea now coordinates Louise's entire healthcare plan. She and Louise have become great friends.

In my book *Authentic Success*, I wrote about the power of readiness and how it can help you to experience a new level of success in every area of your life. In the chapter on *Grace*, I offered this meditation on readiness:

When the student is ready, the teacher appears.

When the thinker is ready, the idea appears.

When the artist is ready, the inspiration appears.

When the servant is ready, the purpose appears.

When the athlete is ready, the performance appears.

When the leader is ready, the vision appears.

When the lover is ready, the partner appears.

When the disciple is ready, God appears.

When the teacher is ready, the student appears.

Receiving is the best psychotherapy. If you're really serious about receiving and you're willing to make it a daily practice, you'll find that receiving will help dissolve all your barriers to love. By declaring *I am willing to be a better receiver,* you activate a power within you that can heal learned unworthiness, dysfunctional independence, unhealthy sacrifice, financial insecurity, and every type of lack. Receiving helps you to know your true worth and to live with ease and happiness.

Receiving helps you to be present. It helps you to be where you are, to inhale deeply, and to take in everything that is here for you. "Often what's missing in a situation is only our ability to receive," says Louise. "The Universe always provides, but we have to be open and receptive to see this." The willingness to receive opens you up inside and takes you beyond your theories of what you believe you deserve and what you think is possible. Receiving helps you to pay attention to what is already here for you.

In this chapter, our spiritual practice is to keep a receiving journal. We invite you to spend 15 minutes a day, for the next seven days, cultivating an even greater willingness to receive. In your receiving journal, we want you to write down ten responses to the sentence *One way life is loving me right now is . . .* Don't edit your responses. Just let them flow.

You may wish to do this exercise with a therapist, a friend, your partner, or your children. You can make it into a dialogue and take turns completing the sentence. Once you have written down your ten responses, review your list and let it sink in how life is loving you right now.

One way life is loving me right now is . . . My wife, Hollie, and I have been doing this exercise together at night when the children are asleep and we have a moment to ourselves. We've been doing it all the way through the writing of *Life Loves You.* This exercise has opened our eyes. On good days, it makes everything sweeter. On difficult days, it lifts our spirits. The more you do this exercise, the easier it is. The more you look, the more you see. As our friend Chuck Spezzano says,

When the receiver is ready,
the gift appears.

CHAPTER 7

Healing the Future

*Every thought we think is
creating our future.*

LOUISE HAY

L ouise and I are sitting down to dinner. We've
spent the whole day talking, walking, gardening,
and doing lots of cooking. We had no plans; we
just went with the flow. It's one of those days that can't
be measured by time. It happened fast and slow. We're
sitting at the edge of the universe—the big round dining table that Louise painted full of stars and swirling
galaxies. The sun is setting over the sea. A humming-
bird is drinking from a fountain in Louise's garden.

"What do you think about the friendly-universe idea?" I ask Louise. She pauses for a moment as she lets the question sink in. "I think it's a good idea," she says with a smile.

The story goes that Albert Einstein once said that the most basic question we all must answer is, "Is the universe a friendly place?" Einstein was a theoretical physicist. He said he wanted to know the thoughts of God. He recognized an "intelligence manifested in Nature" and a "marvelous structure behind reality." He saw the universe as a "unified whole" and the world as an expression of a "lawful harmony" that supports everyone and everything equally. "God is subtle, but he is not malicious," Einstein wrote.

"Is the universe friendly?" I ask Louise.

"There's only one way to find out," she says.

"What way is that?"

"Say yes," she says with a smile.

"What do you mean?"

"If you answer no, you'll never find out if the universe is friendly," she says.

"Because if you say no you won't see it."

"Exactly. But if you say yes then you might."

"It's all in the answer."

"The answer is in us," says Louise.

Louise's answer reminds me of Pascal's Wager. Blaise Pascal was a 17th-century French physicist and philosopher. Meditating on the question of whether God exists, he recognized that reason was of no use here: we can't see non-physical reality—atoms or our own soul. "God is, or He is not," said Pascal. What we must do, he concluded, is wager. In other words, we must decide to say yes or no to the existence of God. He recommended that we wager without hesitation that God exists. "If you gain, you gain all. If you lose, you lose nothing," he said.

Once a week, I host a radio program for Hay House Radio called *Shift Happens!* On a recent show, a woman called in wanting help with finding a romantic partner. She had divorced her husband six-and-a-half years ago and had been on her own ever since. "Does love even exist?" she asked me. I told her, "If you wait for love, you'll never find out." If all we do is wait, we end up like Vladimir and Estragon, the two characters in Samuel Beckett's absurdist play *Waiting for Godot*, who don't even know what they're waiting for. Only by loving will we know if love exists or not.

"Life is always trying to love us, but we need to be open if we are to see it," Louise tells me.

"How do we stay open?" I ask.

"By being willing to love yourself," she says.

"Loving yourself is the key to letting life love you," I tell her.

"When you project your lack of self-love onto others you accuse them of not loving you enough, and all you see is an unfriendly universe," Louise explains.

"'Projection makes perception,'" I say, sharing a line from *A Course in Miracles*.

"Fear shows us one world; and love shows us another world," says Louise. "We decide which world is real. And we decide which world we want to live in."

Albert Einstein also said, "Whether you can observe a thing or not depends on the theory which you use. It is the theory which decides what can be observed." What we see depends on how we look. Einstein encouraged us to burst open our mind so as to escape the prison of our own ideas. He used his intellect, but he warned us not to make the intellect into a god because of its limitations. "I believe in intuitions and inspirations," he said. He also famously said, "Imagination is more important than knowledge. Knowledge is limited. Imagination embraces the entire world."

Philosophers and schools of philosophy throughout history have explored theories and ideas related to the friendly-universe theory. For instance, Plato referred to an Essential Universe and a Perceived Universe. He said that the Essential Universe is perfect, good, and whole (just like your Unconditioned Self). He recognized, however, that the ego (the sense of a separate self) can't see the whole picture, and so it lives in a Perceived Universe, and it's here that we often lose sight of what he called the "absolute beauty" and "friendly harmony" of creation.

Thomas Jefferson was a farmer, a lawyer, and a politician. In his youth, he studied mathematics, metaphysics, and philosophy. As well as being president of the United States, he was also president of the American Philosophical Society. He saw in creation a "benevolent arrangement of things" that influenced much of his thinking. He described God as a "benevolent governor" of the world. He referred to Jesus's work as "the most sublime and benevolent code of morals which has ever been offered to man," that, if followed, would help everyone, without exception, to experience full and free liberty.

A benevolent universe is also at the heart of Buddhist philosophy. The Buddha taught about a universal friendliness and loving-kindness that is the essential consciousness of creation. "Life is a good teacher and a good friend," says Pema Chödrön. This natural benevolence is expressed through each of us when we are aligned with our Unconditioned Self. We lose sight of this benevolence, however, when we stop practicing loving-kindness. And then we suffer.

The recognition of suffering is also at the heart of Buddhism. "Life is full of suffering," says the first of the Four Noble Truths. Nowhere does the Buddha say that life wants us to suffer. The Buddha pointed to the cause of suffering coming not from life but from us. He taught us that we suffer because of what we do to ourselves and what we do to each other. Through loving-kindness and compassion we experience healing and are reunited with the natural harmony of the universe.

"If the universe is friendly, why do we suffer?" I ask Louise.

"Well, I don't believe the universe wants us to suffer," she says.

"And yet there is suffering."

"We heal suffering by identifying the cause of suffering," she says.

"So, what causes us to suffer?" I ask.

"Well, if we are honest with ourselves, we have to accept that we cause a lot of suffering ourselves," she says.

"Life isn't judging us," I say, referring to our earlier conversation.

"Exactly," says Louise. "Life doesn't judge us, but we judge ourselves. Life doesn't criticize us, but we criticize ourselves. Life doesn't abandon us, but we often abandon ourselves. "

"How else do we cause our own suffering?" I ask.

"When we stop loving ourselves, we cause ourselves endless suffering," she says.

We cause ourselves to suffer in 10,000 ways, mostly from a lack of self-love. When we stop loving ourselves, we stop being kind to ourselves. The loss of compassion silences the wisdom of the heart. No kindness, no wisdom. We follow the way of fear. We look for love in all the wrong places. We search for happiness outside ourselves. We chase after success but never feel like we have it. We make a million dollars, but we still feel poor. A million dollars is not enough because it's not two million dollars and because money can't buy what we're really looking for.

"We also cause each other to suffer," says Louise. It's true, isn't it? When people stop loving themselves, they stop loving others, too. That's the way it works. *Hurt people hurt people,* as the old saying goes. When we forget about what's real—the unified whole, our basic truth, the benevolent way of things—we fall from grace and get lost in 10,000 useless dramas. We project our pain, we blame each other, we defend and attack, and we try to win every argument by force. "Only love ends all arguments," says Rumi.

There is another kind of suffering, too. It's the suffering we all experience because of the impermanent nature of life. We mourn the death of loved ones, we lament the end of a relationship, we grieve the loss of a job, and we bear 10,000 other losses. We experience physical pain, illness, old age, and the fear of our own death. The Buddha referred to this suffering as *dukkha*. It comes from grasping at what we want, pushing away what we don't want, wishing everything, including ourselves, would last forever, and forgetting our true nature. This attachment is utterly human, and it deserves our compassion and our love. Love is the cessation of suffering.

"There is another way to look at the friendly-universe theory," Louise says.

"What way is that?" I ask.

"Instead of asking yourself, *How friendly is the universe?* you could ask yourself, *How friendly am I?*" she says with a smile.

"I like that," I say as I let it sink in.

"We are not separate from the universe," she says.

"The universe isn't *out there*," I say, pointing to Louise's dinner table.

"The universe is us," she says.

"And how we are being is how we experience the universe," I add.

"The more we love ourselves, the more we can love each other," says Louise.

"This is how we know that life loves us," I suggest.

"And how we know that the universe really is friendly," Louise says.

Trusting in Love

On the day I started to write this book something extraordinary happened that I can't properly explain. It was such a surprise, and so delightful, that it gave me all the faith I needed for the journey before me.

I had planned to start writing on January 21, but I actually started on January 20, the day before I thought I was ready! I woke up that morning thinking I was going to do some more preparation before the Big Day when I was due to sit in front of a blank page. Page number one. The Alpha page. The OMG page. The page you have to write before you can get to page number two. During my morning meditation, however, I received an internal memo that said, cryptically, "You were born ready. Begin today."

Over breakfast, I told Hollie and Bo and Christopher that I was going to start writing *Life Loves You* that day. "I got a feeling that it would be good to start before I was ready," I told Hollie. Hollie smiled. Christopher chewed on a pancake. Bo got up from the table and ran upstairs. Two minutes later, she came back with a rose quartz crystal angel in her hands. "Here you are, Daddy," she said. "Put her on your desk and she will help you write." Christopher jumped out of his seat. He came back with his favorite tractor. "Here, Daddy," he said. "This tractor will be a big help."

Later that morning, I sat at my desk looking at the blank page. Page number one. The pink angel was standing next to the computer screen. The tractor was downstairs. Christopher had changed his mind about that. "You can have my tractor, Daddy, but only if I can keep it," he told me. Now the spirit of the tractor was with me, parked right next to the angel. Also on my desk was a jasmine-scented candle, a cup of Kona coffee, and a card with one of my favorite messages from *A Course in Miracles*:

It cannot be that it is hard to do
the task that Christ appointed you to do,
since it is He Who does it.

As I stared at the blank page, an image came to mind of a painting of Jesus Christ standing at a door holding a lantern in his left hand. I'd seen this painting before, but I wasn't sure where. This image of Christ was all I could think about. I convinced myself that a mystical vision was a valid reason to delay writing and do a search on Google. I typed "Paintings of Jesus Christ," clicked on the Images tab, and there, at the top of the page, was the painting I was looking for: *The Light of the World*, by William Holman Hunt.

When I saw the painting, I remembered that I'd had a dream about it the night before. I don't remember many of my dreams, and I can't tell you much about this one. I simply remember that I dreamed about that painting. Maybe that was why it appeared on my blank page. Anyway, I took it as a sign that "unseen hands," as Joseph Campbell described, were helping me on my way. I bookmarked some articles about the painting to read later. I also downloaded an image of the painting to use on my computer as a screen saver. At the moment, however, I needed to get back to the blank page. Page number one.

Meanwhile, Hollie was downstairs in the kitchen. Something was on her mind, too. She was looking for a gift of some kind to help me with my writing. The way Hollie describes it, her body marched her upstairs and into her office. She scanned the room. Her eyes fell upon a picture that was resting on a bookshelf. She hadn't noticed the picture before. She didn't know anything about it. She assumed it belonged to me. She put the picture in a silver oval frame and then came upstairs to see me. "Close your eyes and put out your hands," Hollie said. "I have something for you."

When I opened my eyes, I was looking at a framed picture of *The Light of the World,* by William Holman Hunt. How did this happen? I was astonished. Hollie was "weirded out," as she put it. Hollie often brings me gifts when I write—smoothies, green juices, and home-baked muffins, but not this. "Hi, honey, here's a religious icon" isn't normal for us. Neither of us had any prior knowledge of this painting. Now it's the first thing I see when I turn on my computer. And the framed picture sits next to the pink angel and the spirit of the tractor.

When I told Louise this story, she smiled. It was one of her knowing smiles. "I experienced so many little miracles and coincidences when I wrote *You Can Heal Your Life*," she told me. "I had the strongest feeling that I shouldn't go to a mainstream publisher, even though I'd had some offers. I felt like I was the custodian of important information that mustn't be edited or watered down. I had no idea how to self-publish, but I trusted the process, and doors opened for me every step of the way."

Shortly after speaking to Louise, I stumbled across this affirmation by Florence Scovel Shinn: *All doors now open for happy surprises, and the Divine Plan of my life is speeded up under grace.*

The Light of the World by William Holman Hunt is inspired by two verses in the Bible. At the foot of the painting is an inscription from Revelation 3:20. It reads: "Behold, I stand at the door and knock. If any man hears my voice and opens the door, I will come in to him and eat with him and he with me." The title of the painting is from John 8:12, in which Jesus says, "I am the light of the world. Whoever follows me will never walk in darkness, but will have the light of life." Both verses call upon the ego to be open and receptive to holy guidance and a higher plan.

Hunt's painting is full of symbolism and allegory. Christ represents our Unconditioned Self. The door represents our ego mind. Christ's face is a picture of infinite patience. Weeds grow at the foot of the door, which tells us that the door has been shut for some time. Hunt described the symbolism: "The closed door was the obstinately shut mind, the weeds the cumber of daily neglect . . ." Most significant, the door has no handle, no lock, and no bolt. It can be opened at any moment. It opens from the inside. Our soul waits for us. Our ego must be willing to let the light in. Our ego has to open the door.

"Once I took my first step on the spiritual path, I felt like I walked through a door into a new world," Louise tells me as we sit looking at Hunt's painting. "Life took me by the hand and led me on my way. Life said, 'Do this,' and I did. Life said, 'Do that,' and I did. When people want to know how I created Hay House, I always tell them, 'I opened my mind. I listened to my inner voice. I followed the signs. I trusted the flow and learned to move with it.'"

"I have faith in the universe," said Albert Einstein to William Hermanns in a conversation recorded in *Einstein and the Poet*. This book is one of my favorites about Einstein. It features four conversations between

Einstein and Hermanns, a German poet, playwright, and sociologist, over the space of thirty years. Einstein tells Hermanns, "Through my pursuit in science I have known cosmic religious feelings." Einstein insists he is a scientist, but he also sounds like a poet. He makes reference to an inner voice. And he tells Hermanns, "If I hadn't an absolute faith in the harmony of creation, I wouldn't have tried for 30 years to express it in a mathematical formula."

"When you know that life loves you, and that you live in a friendly universe, it helps you in both the good times and the bad times," says Louise. Sometimes life doesn't go according to plan. Not to our plan, at least. We all know what that's like. We feel like life loves us when we get what we want, but what about when we don't? What about when we don't get that job we wanted? Or when that special person doesn't return our call? Or when something that felt so right goes wrong? This is when we have to trust that life loves us *always*—and that even when things appear not to be going our way, they still are going our way.

"If you knew Who walks beside you on the way that you have chosen, fear would be impossible," states *A Course in Miracles*. When we're afraid, we feel alone. *When one door closes all the other doors close, too,* is how it feels to our ego. "When you trust in love, it's impossible to feel totally alone," says Louise. "Love introduces you to the totality of possibilities. It opens you up to a power that is greater and wiser than your ego. Love knows what's best for you. It leads you to your highest good. Love will show you the way."

Whenever you feel stuck, lonely, or afraid, Louise and I recommend you ask yourself this question: *What good things could happen if I let life love me even more?* Another way of doing this is to complete this sentence ten times: *One way I could let life love me even more right now is . . .* Open the door and let your soul lead the way. Open your mind and let the light in. Open your heart and trust in love to take you where you need to go. To support you in this inquiry here is one of my favorite passages by Louise from her book *Heart Thoughts:*

Trust that your inner guide is
leading you and guiding you in ways
that are best for you, and that your
spiritual growth is continuously
expanding.

No matter which door opens or
which door closes, you
are always safe.

You are eternal.
You will go on forever
from experience to experience.
See yourself opening doors to
joy, peace, healing, prosperity,
and love.

Doors to understanding,
compassion, and forgiveness.
Doors to freedom. Doors to
self-worth and self-esteem.
Doors to self-love.

It is all here before you.
Which door will you open first?
Remember, you are safe;
it is only change.

Teach Only Love

One afternoon, Louise and I took a walk in Balboa
Park. We stopped off at Daniel's Coffee Cart to pick
up my cappuccino. From there, we headed to the Japanese Friendship Garden. As we walked, I ask Louise
about the Hayride Reunion that had just taken place. It

celebrated the 30th anniversary of Louise's support group for AIDS that became known as the Hayride. The Reunion was held at the Wilshire Ebell Theatre in Los Angeles. The theater was full of friends old and new who came from all over the world to be there.

Suddenly we heard someone shout, "Ms. Hay! Ms. Hay!" We looked up and saw two men, arm in arm, waving at us. They were by the entrance to the Japanese Friendship Garden. As they approached, one of the men said, "Ms. Hay, I'm a Hayrider!" Louise and the man both burst into tears. They hugged each other for a long time. I took lots of pictures. Louise looked so happy. This man had attended Hayride meetings back in 1988 when he was preparing to die. "You healed my life," he said. "No. *You* healed your life," Louise told him.

Louise hosted a Hayride every Wednesday night for six-and-a-half years in the 1980s. "A private client asked me if I'd hold a meeting for men with AIDS. I said yes. That's how it began," Louise told me. Six men showed up for the first meeting, which Louise held in her living room. "I told the men that we were going to do what I always do, which is to focus on self-love, forgiveness, and letting go of fear. I also told them that we were not going to sit there and play *Ain't it awful*, because that won't help anybody." At the end of the first meeting, Louise and her six men held each other in a loving embrace. They left Louise's home that night with a feeling of peace in their hearts.

"The week after, we had 12 men sitting in my living room. The following week, we had 20 men. And it just kept growing," Louise says, still astonished by what happened. "Eventually, we had nearly 90 men squeezed into my living room. I'm not sure what the neighbors thought! Each week we talked, we cried, we sang songs together, we did mirror work and also all sorts of healing meditations for ourselves, each other, and the planet. We ended every evening with hugs, which was good for love, *and also very good for pick-ups,*" says Louise with a big smile.

The meetings moved out of Louise's home into a gymnasium in West Hollywood. "We went from 90 people to 150 people that first night," she recalls. They soon had to move again. This time the City of West Hollywood gave Louise a space that could hold hundreds of people. "Eventually, we had nearly 800 people at our Wednesday night meetings. Now it wasn't just men with AIDS who came. It was men and women. And family members, too. Whenever someone's mother attended her first meeting, she'd receive a standing ovation from us all."

One of Louise's closest friends is Daniel Peralta. They first met in January 1986, when Daniel attended the premiere of a film about the Hayride called *Doors Opening: A Positive Approach to AIDS.* "Louise Hay introduced me to unconditional love," Daniel told me. In an article about the Hayride, Daniel wrote about Louise's infinite kindness and her generosity of spirit:

> Louise L. Hay was ushering in a new possibility, a new way of being. She introduced us to loving ourselves and outlined practical steps to engage that process. She gently invited us to be with ourselves in a new and different way, and practice self-acceptance and self-care. Not only was it appealing, it was healing. I clearly remember how Louise had this incredible ability to quickly create a sense of community and bring people together, one heart at a time.

Louise cries freely when she talks about the Hayrides. "These young people were terrified and lonely. They'd been rejected by their family and by society," Louise tells me. "What they needed was a friend—someone who wasn't afraid, who wouldn't judge them, and who loved them for who they are. I simply answered the call." When I ask Louise about her tears, she says, "We got through a lot of Kleenex at the Hayride. I made so many friends. I lost a lot of friends, too. We attended far too many funerals. But we also made sure no one died without knowing they were loved. And, of course, many people lived on and created a future they never expected to have."

In the opening sequence of *Doors Opening*, Louise says, "I don't heal anybody. I just provide a space where we can uncover how absolutely wonderful we are, and many people find that they're able to heal themselves." Louise is consistent in her message. I've witnessed hundreds of people tell Louise personally, "Thank you for healing my life." I smile every time it happens because I know how Louise will respond. "*You* healed your life," she tells them.

"Louise, people have called you a lot of things," I say.

"I know," she says, laughing.

"You tell everyone, *I am not a healer.*"

"That's right," she says firmly.

"So what are you?"

"Oh, I don't know."

"You've been called a living saint."

"Well, I can't help that," she says, clearly embarrassed.

"Oprah Winfrey called you the Mother of the Law of Attraction."

"Uh-huh."

"You've been called a guru and a pioneer."

"Uh-huh."

"And a rebel."

"Oh, I like that," she says, laughing.

"Have you ever painted a self-portrait?" I ask her.

"Never!"

"Come on, Louise: tell me who you are."

"Well, how would *you* describe me?"

"I have a couple of ideas."

"I'll take them both!"

"I think you're a lioness," I tell her.

"Well, I have Leo rising in my chart," she says.

"I think you're fierce about the truth."

"Fierce and direct," she says.

"You're also very protective of the people you love."

"Extremely," she says.

"I also think you're a teacher," I tell her.

"That's true," she says.

When I think about Louise and her work, there's a line from *A Course in Miracles* that immediately springs to mind: "Teach only love, for that is what you are."

Louise is a teacher, and she teaches about love. She teaches that in every given moment of your life you are choosing between love and fear, love and pain, and love and hate. "I teach one thing—and one thing only—love yourself," says Louise.

"Until you love yourself, you will never know who you really are and you won't know what you're really capable of," Louise told me on a recent Skype call. She sees love as the miracle ingredient that helps you to grow into the person you truly are. "When you love yourself, you grow up," she says. "Love helps you to grow beyond your past, beyond pain, beyond fears, beyond your ego, and beyond all your small ideas about yourself. Love is what you're made of, and love helps you to be who you really are."

One of the great joys of being Louise's friend is witnessing her passion and commitment for growth. Louise Hay loves to learn. "If I hadn't learned to love myself, none of what I've done since would have been possible," she tells me. Louise's message is, *Love yourself now. Don't wait until you're ready.* "If you won't love yourself today, you won't love yourself tomorrow either. But if you start today, you begin to create a better future, and your future self will be so grateful to you," she says.

Louise is always on the lookout for new growth and new adventures. After her first public art exhibit, she wrote a post on Facebook saying, "Life goes in cycles. There's a time to do something new, and then there's a time to move on. It's never too late to learn something new." After the Hayride Reunion, she told me, "I feel like one door has closed and another door is opening now. I am open and receptive to new opportunities to grow." On our most recent Skype call, Louise told me she has signed up for a course on spiritual homeopathy.

While we've been writing *Life Loves You,* Louise has felt as if she's on the threshold of a whole new chapter in her life. She told me that she has no idea what this new chapter is about yet. She said, "I feel excited and nervous, but I remind myself each day that life loves me, that I'm safe, that life wants the best for me, and that it's only change." When I asked Louise how she planned to welcome in her new chapter, she said, "I'm going to rearrange some furniture. I'll let go of a few things, and I'll make room for the new."

Recently, I gave the opening keynote for the IGNITE! conference hosted by Hay House UK in London. The conference featured 12 authors talking about personal growth and global transformation. I asked Louise if she had a message she'd like to share with the audience. She promptly shot me an e-mail full of passion and high teaching. Here's what she asked me to share:

I ignite my life every time I do something new.
Daring to step into new space is so exciting.
I know that only good lies before me
so I am ready for whatever Life has in store for me.
New adventures keep us young.
And sending loving thoughts in every direction
keeps our lives filled with love.
87 is the new beginning of my life.

A Loving Mirror

When Louise Hay walks onto the stage at an I Can Do It! conference, the audience rises to its feet in spontaneous appreciation. Thousands of people join as one to shower Louise with love and thanks. It happens every time, all over the world, in cities like Vancouver, London, New York, Sydney, and Hamburg, Germany. I've stood in those audiences on many occasions, and I've been moved to tears pretty much each time. It's wonderful to think about what can happen in this world when one person makes a stand for love.

This time Louise and I are in Denver for another I Can Do It! We're in Louise's hotel room, reviewing the early chapters of this book. "The message I most want our readers to hear is *Life loves you as you are, and it wants you to do the same,*" Louise tells me. "We're here on this planet to learn about unconditional love, and it begins with self-acceptance and self-love." Pointing her finger at me, she says, "In your life you have to start with loving you." She then points to herself and says, "And in my life I have to start with loving me." She pauses for a moment and then says, "And that's how we love the world."

When you teach about self-love, like Louise and I do, you quickly get used to dealing with any number of objections and concerns. The common ones include "Self-love is selfish"; "Self-love is self-indulgent"; "Self-love is narcissistic." Is this really true? My feeling is that narcissism is narcissistic, but self-love isn't narcissism. In other words, most of the objections to self-love come from misperceptions of what love is. "Self-love is not about vanity or arrogance, it's about self-respect," says Louise. "It's a deep appreciation for how you've been made and for the life you are here to live."

In my *Loveability* program, I tell my students who are afraid that self-love is selfish to take a look at Louise

Hay's life. Louise's story is a wonderful example of how self-healing and self-love can be a blessing for others. Look what happened after Louise embarked on her healing journey. She wrote the first version of her little blue book, entitled *What Hurts*, when she was 50 years old. Three years later, she rewrote the book and published it as *Heal Your Body*. When Louise was 56 years old, she started the Hayride. She set up her charity, the Hay Foundation, when she was 59 years old. She founded Hay House when she was 60 years old. All this, and she was just getting started.

"We are here to be a loving mirror to the world," Louise tells me. The more we love ourselves, the less we project our pain onto the world. When we stop judging ourselves, we naturally judge others less. When we stop attacking ourselves, we don't attack others. When we stop rejecting ourselves, we stop accusing others of hurting us. When we start loving ourselves more, we become happier, less defended, and more open. As we love ourselves, we naturally love others more. "Self-love is the greatest gift because what you give yourself is experienced by others," says Louise.

When I founded The Happiness Project in 1994, I created a mission statement that was just two words:

Talk happiness. Back then, there wasn't much talk about happiness in psychology or in society. The goal of The Happiness Project was to stimulate a conversation about happiness. We talked about happiness in schools, hospitals, churches, businesses, and in halls of government. The more we talked, the more I learned about what happiness is, and the more convinced I became that happiness, like self-love, benefits both self and society. After a few years, I created a new mission statement for The Happiness Project. It reads:

It is because the world is so full of suffering
that your happiness is a gift.
It is because the world is so full of poverty
that your wealth is a gift.
It is because the world is so unfriendly
that your smile is a gift.
It is because the world is so full of war
that your peace of mind is a gift.
It is because the world is in such despair
that your hope and optimism is a gift.
It is because the world is so afraid
that your love is a gift.

Love is always shared. It's a gift, like true happiness and success. It ends up benefiting you and others. "When

I think about love, I like to visualize myself standing in a circle of light," says Louise. "This circle represents love, and I see myself surrounded by love. Once I feel this love in my heart and in my body, I see the circle expanding to fill the room, and then every square inch of my home, and then the neighborhood, and then the whole city, and then the whole country, and then the whole planet, and eventually, the whole universe. That's how love is, to me. That's how love works."

Listening to Louise talk about her circle of love reminds me of these words by Albert Einstein: "A human being is a part of the whole, called by us 'Universe,' a part limited in time and space. We experience ourselves, our thoughts, and feelings as something separate from the rest. A kind of optical delusion of consciousness. This delusion is a kind of prison for us, restricting us to our personal desires and to affection for a few persons nearest to us. Our task must be to free ourselves from this prison by widening our circle of compassion to embrace all living creatures and the whole of nature in its beauty."

When Louise Hay founded Hay House in 1987, she told everyone who came to work with her that the purpose of the publishing company was not just to sell books and tapes. "Of course, I wanted us to be financially successful, so that we could pay wages and look after everyone, but I also had a higher vision," Louise tells me. "What I knew then, and still believe today, is that the real purpose of Hay House is to help *create a world where it is safe for us to love each other*. With each book we print, we bless the world with love."

PRACTICE 7:
BLESSING THE WORLD

When Louise last appeared on *The Oprah Winfrey Show*, she had recently celebrated her 81st birthday, and she told Oprah that she'd just taken up lessons in ballroom dancing. When Oprah asked Louise what advice she had for anyone who thinks it's too late to change and grow, Louise responded empathically, "Rethink! Just because you've believed something for a long time doesn't mean you have to think it forever. Think thoughts that support you and uplift you. Realize that life loves you. And if you love life, you get this wonderful thing going."

Getting this "wonderful thing going," as Louise puts it, isn't just about letting life love you; it's also about you loving life. When Louise and I met for the first time to discuss this book, I told her that I wanted to explore the full meaning of her philosophy *Life loves you*. Here's what she had to say: "To experience what *Life loves you* really means, I recommend you say this affirmation to yourself: *Life loves me, and I love life.* You can change it around if you like: *I love life, and life loves me.* This is what I say to myself every day, and I intend to say it every day for the rest of my life." This affirmation is the inspiration for our seventh and final spiritual practice for you.

When you affirm *Life loves me, and I love life,* you paint in your consciousness an unbroken circle of receiving and giving. *Life loves me* represents the receiving principle, and *I love life* represents the giving principle. The full affirmation supports you in receiving and giving love in equal measure. In truth, giving *is* receiving. The giver and the receiver are the same person. What you give, you receive. And what you receive, you can give. This awareness is what helps you to be a truly loving presence in the world.

Your spiritual practice for this chapter is a meditation called *Blessing the World*. It is inspired by the Buddhist practice of *mettā*, which is a Pali word for *loving-kindness, universal friendship, benevolence.* The meditation has five parts to it. We recommend you take between 5 and 15 minutes to do this practice. As with the other practices in the book, Louise and I encourage you to do this once a day for seven consecutive days. The more you do it, the better it gets.

Blessing Yourself: "There is enough love in you to love the whole planet, and it starts with you," says Louise. Begin by affirming *Life loves me, and I love life.* Say it out loud. Say it a few times. Complete the sentence *One way life is loving me right now is . . .* Count your blessings. If you find this difficult, affirm that you are willing to receive and that you are open to all offers of help. Affirm *Today I move into my greater good. My good is everywhere, and I am safe and secure.*

Blessing Loved Ones: Wish everyone you love a beautiful day today. Affirm for them *Life loves you.* Pray that they may know how blessed they are and that they recognize the basic truth about themselves, which is *I am loveable.* Be happy for their success, their abundance, their good health, and their good fortune. "Remember, if you want love and acceptance from your family, then you must have love and acceptance for them," says Louise. Affirm *I rejoice in everyone's happiness, knowing that there is plenty for us all.*

Blessing Your Neighborhood: Set up in your mind that you will bless everyone you meet today. Send a blessing to all your neighbors on both sides of the street. Send a blessing to all the parents you normally see at the school gate. Send a blessing to the local shop-keeper, to the mailman, to the bus driver, and to every other familiar face in your community. Send a blessing to the trees on your street. Send a blessing to your entire neighborhood. Affirm *Life loves you, and I wish you infinite blessings today.*

Bless Your Enemies: Send a blessing to the people you're tempted to withhold love from. Bless the person you judge the most and affirm *Life loves us all.* Bless the person you fight with the most and affirm *Life loves us all.* Bless the person you complain about the most and affirm *Life loves us all.* Bless the person you envy the most and affirm *Life loves us all.* Bless the person you compete with the most and affirm *Life loves us all.* Bless your enemies, so that you have no enemies. Affirm *We are all loveable. Life loves us all. In love, everyone wins.*

Bless the World: Affirm *Life loves me, and I love life.* Imagine that you hold the whole planet in your heart. "You are important, and what you do with your mind makes a difference. Send out a blessing to the whole world every day," says Louise. Love the animals. Love the plants. Love the oceans. Love the stars. Visualize newspaper headlines like "A Cure for Cancer," or "An End to Poverty," or "Peace on Earth." Each time you bless the world with your love, you connect with millions of people doing the same thing. See the world evolving in the direction of love today. Affirm *Together we are creating a world in which it is safe to love one another.*

Postscript

Today, I've been working on the final edit of the manuscript for *Life Loves You*. Christopher has been playing in my office with his new tractor. He's so happy. "It's the best tractor in the universe, Dad," he tells me. His old tractor sits on my desk now, next to the angel Bo gave me and the picture of Christ holding the lantern. Hollie and I are still amazed at how this picture appeared in our home.

This morning I was thumbing through my copy of *You Can Heal Your Life*. I was checking a quote for accuracy. It's a well-worn copy, several years old now, and I've only just noticed that Louise has inscribed it. The inscription reads, "Remember, 'life loves you.' Tee Hee. Love to Robert. Louise Hay." The *Tee Hee* is underlined for emphasis. *Why did Louise write Tee Hee?* I wonder. Did she know something I didn't? I smile in gratitude for the journey we have taken together.

My sciatica has healed now. I am free of "sensations," as Louise puts it. My physiotherapist gave me a clean bill of health a few weeks ago. The timing of the sciatica was symbolic. It began just a few days before I started to write this book. Another coincidence! In *You Can Heal Your Life*, Louise describes the probable cause of sciatica as *hypocrisy*. When I looked closely at this, I found the place in me where I believe that life loves me, but I also found shadows, doubts, fears, cynicism, and unworthiness.

Life Loves You is a big inquiry. Louise and I took our dialogue as far as we could together. And there's more to go, for both of us. In a recent conversation, Louise told me, "I still get afraid, and sometimes I doubt that life loves me, but it happens less now. I know, deep down, that a fear is *only a fear* and not the truth. When I find a fear, I meet it with love. And I remind myself that life is not judging me or rejecting me. Life loves me."

This book is nearly finished, but it feels like the inquiry has just begun. Each of us has a self-image, an ego, that we hope is loveable, but egos are full of holes. These holes hide buried fears and doubts, and they cast a shadow on the world as we see it. *Life loves you* asks us to dig deep, to excavate the ground of our being, where our true nature lives. Here is our buried treasure. Here is where we meet our Unconditioned Self. This is the Self that life loves.

An inquiry on love is infinite by its nature. Soon Louise and I will work on the online program for *Life Loves You*. We'll create a *Life Loves You* card deck, full of spiritual practices and affirmations. We'll also post a series of interviews on the Heal Your Life website. These offerings will help to take the inquiry even deeper.

The more we let life love us, the more we can be the person we truly are. The inner work, then, is to dissolve the blocks to love and to keep on doing so until only love remains. Love is our true nature. Love is how we express our heart. Love is our soul's purpose. We are here to love the world. We are here to choose love over fear. This is our gift to ourselves and to each other.

Acknowledgments

Robert thanks Louise Hay for saying *Yes* to writing this book together. Thank you, Hollie Holden, for your love and support. Once again, our late-night conversations, after our babies had finally fallen asleep, gave me inspiration and direction for the journey. Thank you, Laura Samuel and Lizzie Prior, for helping me to create the space to write. Thank you, Shelley Anderson and Natasha Fletcher, for your help with research. Thank you again, Dr. David Hamilton, for support regarding science. Thank you, Thomas Newman, for your music, particularly the soundtrack for *Saving Mr. Banks*, which I listened to while I wrote this book. Thank you, Meggan Watterson, for that comment you made at dinner that night with Hollie and me. Thank you to Raina Nahar, Jack Smith, Finn Thomas, and Alan Watson for your support.

Thank you to William Morris Endeavor and my agent, Jennifer Rudolph Walsh.

Robert and Louise also thank the Hay House team for bringing this book to the world. Thank you to Patty Gift, our editor. Thank you also to Leanne Siu Anastasi, Christy Salinas, Joan Oliver, Richelle Zizian, Laura Gray, and Sally Mason.

About the Authors

L ouise Hay, the author of the international best-seller *You Can Heal Your Life,* is a metaphysical lecturer and teacher with more than 50 million books sold worldwide. For more than 30 years, she has helped people throughout the world discover and implement the full potential of their own creative powers for personal growth and self-healing. She has appeared on *The Oprah Winfrey Show* and many other TV and radio programs both in the U.S. and abroad.

Websites: www.LouiseHay.com® and www.HealYour Life.com®

Facebook page: www.Facebook.com/LouiseLHay

Robert Holden, Ph.D.'s innovative work on psychology and spirituality has been featured on *The Oprah Winfrey Show, Good Morning America,* a PBS show called *Shift Happens!,* and a major BBC documentary called *How to Be Happy*, shown in 20 countries to more than 30 million television viewers. He's the author of *Happiness NOW!*, *Shift Happens!*, *Authentic Success* (formerly titled *Success Intelligence*), *Be Happy*, *Loveability*, and *Holy Shift!: 365 Daily Meditations from* A Course in Miracles. He contributes daily to his Facebook page (drrobertholden) and hosts a weekly show for Hay House Radio called *Shift Happens!*

Website: www.robertholden.org

Hay House Titles of Related Interest

YOU CAN HEAL YOUR LIFE, the movie,
starring Louise Hay & Friends
(available as a 1-DVD program and an expanded 2-DVD set)
Watch the trailer at: www.LouiseHayMovie.com

THE SHIFT, the movie, starring Dr. Wayne W. Dyer
(available as a 1-DVD program and an expanded
2-DVD set)
Watch the trailer at: www.DyerMovie.com

*THE ANSWER IS SIMPLE . . . LOVE YOURSELF, LIVE
YOUR SPIRIT!,* by Sonia Choquette

I CAN SEE CLEARLY NOW, by Dr. Wayne W. Dyer

*MIRACLES NOW: 108 Life-Changing Tools for Less
Stress, More Flow, and Finding Your True Purpose,*
by Gabrielle Bernstein

YOU CAN CREATE AN EXCEPTIONAL LIFE
by Louise Hay and Cheryl Richardson

All of the above are available at your local bookstore,
or may be ordered by contacting Hay House (see next page).

We hope you enjoyed this Hay House book. If you'd like to receive our online catalog featuring additional information on Hay House books and products, or if you'd like to find out more about the Hay Foundation, please contact:

Hay House, Inc., P.O. Box 5100, Carlsbad, CA 92018-5100
(760) 431-7695 or (800) 654-5126
(760) 431-6948 (fax) or (800) 650-5115 (fax)
www.hayhouse.com® • www.hayfoundation.org

Published and distributed in Australia by: Hay House Australia Pty. Ltd., 18/36 Ralph St., Alexandria NSW 2015 • *Phone:* 612-9669-4299 • *Fax:* 612-9669-4144 • www.hayhouse.com.au

Published and distributed in the United Kingdom by: Hay House UK, Ltd., Astley House, 33 Notting Hill Gate, London W11 3JQ • *Phone:* 44-20-3675-2450 • *Fax:* 44-20-3675-2451 • www.hayhouse.co.uk

Published and distributed in the Republic of South Africa by: Hay House SA (Pty), Ltd., P.O. Box 990, Witkoppen 2068 • *Phone/Fax:* 27-11-467-8904 • www.hayhouse.co.za

Published in India by: Hay House Publishers India, Muskaan Complex, Plot No. 3, B-2, Vasant Kunj, New Delhi 110 070 • *Phone:* 91-11-4176-1620 • *Fax:* 91-11-4176-1630 • www.hayhouse.co.in

NOTES

NOTES

NOTES

NOTES

NOTES

NOTES

NOTES

NOTES

NOTES